Florence Scovel-Shinn's Game of Life ~ Unleashed ~

Change Your Life for 2012 and Beyond NOW!

Volume I - 2010

Kathryn Speakes-Large
and
Florence Scovel-Shinn

Florence Scovel-Shinn's Game of Life ~ Unleashed ~
Change Your Life for 2012 and Beyond Now!
Volume I - 2010

Waiting in the Other Room Productions
WaitingInTheOtherRoom.com
SoulKisses.com
FlorenceScovelShinnsGameOfLife.com

ISBN -13 978-0-9826061-0-0
ISBN -10 0982606109

Library of Congress Control Number: 2010920692

The Sedona Method® of Release is printed with permission of Sedona Training Associates
Sedona.com

Photos of Kathryn Speakes-Large by Jesse Large of MiaBellaVitaPhotography.com
Cover Photograph by Dreamstime.com/Brian Goodman

The Game of Life Published by arrangement with DeVorss & Company.

Printed in the United States of America

Dedication

This book is dedicated to Florence Scovel Shinn.
Her work "opened the way" to my spiritual path
at a time that I desperately needed it.

Clearly the teacher arrives when the student is ready…

Acknowledgments

The teacher arrives when the student is ready.
Life has been an exciting adventure – the teachers have come and gone in miraculous ways.

Thank you to Sherry Lewis who introduced me to Florence Scovel Shinn's work in the early 90's. Sherry loaned her copy of *The Game of Life* to me and I never gave it back. As a matter of fact, I cut the spine off the book, hole punched the pages and put them into a notebook to access easily when I wrote the e-course *The Keys to Unlocking the Secrets ~ The Game of Life Unleashed!*

Thank you to Barbara Mark who gave me the title for the e-course and ultimately this book – *The Game of Life Unleashed!* Barbara suggested the title from the spirit world where she now resides and continues to bring love and laughter to my life.

Thank you to Jennifer Hoffman for being the beautiful, loving, nonjudgmental, supportive essence that you are. When asked if she thought I could do something, she didn't hesitate, she firmly answered with all the authority that IS Jennifer, "Of course you can!"

Thank you to those of you who experienced the e-course and loved it!

Thank you to those of you who are experiencing this book! May your heart be open to the blessings of enlightenment.

Table of Contents

Introduction

The Game of Life and How to Play It came to me during a very sad, unhappy period of time in my life – I had foolishly given my personal power away and it felt as if my life force was draining from me. Then a miracle occurred. I met a wonderful woman who saw the light of God shining within me trying so desperately to survive the physical world. She asked the angels what she could do to help me and they led her to her bookcase. As she stood there in front of the books, she asked which one to loan to me. *The Game of Life and How to Play It*, by Florence Scovel Shinn fell to the floor.

As I read the words of wisdom Florence shared in the book, I couldn't put it down. What Florence had written seventy years before resonated deep within me. I snatched back my personal power and began to search within me for my true self and I found her. Together with my entourage of angels, guides and teachers, my spiritual journey began in earnest.

The Game of Life is a powerful tool that will only "click" with people when they are ready. In reading it more than once new meaning, new vigor, new strength and power are discovered each time, because with each reading the mind is at a higher level of consciousness.

The workbook brings 1925 terminology into the 21st century and guides us to implementing our connection with God into our daily way of thinking, being and doing.

It is up to us to experience our spiritual journey of enlightenment, to discern our truth and grow spiritually. Florence Scovel Shinn uses real life examples to explain the cause and effect of trusting in God as our supply. Using her examples, this workbook delves deeper into her words and offers tools and experiential exercises to understand and attain a higher level of consciousness.

Make no mistake – after experiencing *The Game of Life* and this workbook, your life will change forever and you will never be able to go back to existing in the dark heavy physically conditioned life you've been living. You will be empowered by your connection with God and the understanding of Universal Laws. You will tap deep within you the limitlessness of your spiritual being and you will develop the tools to become *One with God*. You will learn how to release your physical world conditioned thought patterns and beliefs; thereby opening the limitless doors of possibilities to your life.

This workbook, based on *The Game of Life* explores so much more deeply the dynamics of the Fourth Dimensional Realm and the Universal Laws. **It is dynamite!!**

Contents of this Workbook:

* Workbook: Ten individual experiential sessions broken down by chapter of the book

* Book: The Game of Life and How to Play it

* Journaling pages

Note: The wondrous gift of this Workbook and Florence's work is that each time the material is accessed you will be on a new level of consciousness, therefore, you will experience new and exciting enlightenment and empowerment.

This is an interactive workbook. Take the time you need to work through each session. Be sure to use the journaling pages. As you work your way through the workbook, refer back to the experiences of the exercises that you have written about. This is a powerful tool to understand how quickly you've elevated your consciousness – your spiritual connection and how amazingly you've opened the doors to miraculous blessings.

You will see as you progress, that the things that were perhaps a little confusing become clear or clearer. After some time has passed, experience the workbook again – you will be amazed at how much *more* you will learn, understand and experience!

The journaling is an extremely valuable tool!! There will be times that you'll think – I'll do the journaling later – STOP! Don't allow yourself to be sucked back into the physical world "to do's" yet! Take a few minutes – even if it is only five minutes, to write about your experience. This step is as important as the processes of the workbook – as you progress through the workbook and book, your journal will help you to anchor your spiritual growth. Again, don't skip the journaling – you will be cheating yourself if you do!

About Florence Scovel Shinn

While living in the physical world Florence Scovel Shinn was widely known for many years as an artist and illustrator, metaphysician and lecturer, who helped thousands of people through her great work of healing and assisting in solving their problems.

She is the author of *The Game of Life and How to Play It, Your Word is Your Wand,* and *The Secret Door to Success. The Power of the Spoken Word* was published after her death in 1945.

Florence crossed over October 17, 1940.

In the late summer of 2006 she came to me and wanted to create an e-course based on *The Game of Life and How to Play It.* This was an exciting time for me, learning more about her and how she wanted to continue to serve the peoples of Mother Earth.

She chose what chapter we worked on and I dutifully carried out her wishes typing up the course and creating the experiential forms. When we had three chapters left I hit a roadblock. It was as if she deserted me. I connected with my guides and learned that I had life experiences to work through before we could finish. The life experiences were painful. Once they were complete, Florence came back and we finished the e-course in 2007.

I found her to be an amazing spirit of love, light and joy. I'm sure you will too as you read through our work. Don't be surprised if you find her "reminding" you how powerful your thoughts are at times when you least expect it.

Directions to use the Workbook

The workbook includes Florence's book *The Game of Life*. You will read a chapter of *The Game of Life* then you will move into the subsequent session of the workbook.

Journaling sections are included within the workbook sessions after each experiential exercise. A journaling section follows each workbook session allowing you to record and anchor your experiences.

Take your time as you move through the workbook. Some sections will be easier than others. All will flow and miraculous blessings will unfold as you work in tandem with your angelic entourage to lift the veil of confusion and embrace all that is yours by divine right.

Again, the journaling is extremely valuable due to its power of anchoring your growth and opening the way to the rememberings of who you are deep within – a limitless spiritual being whose Field of Potentiality is equally limitless. Take the time to journal!

Repetition with Purpose

We are beings of conditioned layers of fear. As we evolve and grow a new layer of fear is revealed to us. The work of Florence Scovel Shinn helps us to peal back these layers, resolve, heal and dissipate the fear, thereby, ascending in our evolution of mind, body and spirit.

With each chapter of *The Game of Life* and the workbook we uncover new layers. Each time the workbook is opened after completing it, new layers are revealed. We are as an onion…

Chapter 1 - The Game

It is a game, however, which cannot be played successfully without the knowledge of spiritual law, and the Old and the New Testaments give the rules of the game with wonderful clearness. Jesus Christ taught that it was a great game of *Giving and Receiving.*

Whatsoever a man soweth that shall he also reap." This means that whatever man sends out in word or deed, will return to him; what he gives, he will receive.

If he gives hate, he will receive hate; if he gives love, he will receive love; if he gives criticism, he will receive criticism; if he lies he will be lied to; if he cheats he will be cheated. We are taught also, that the imaging faculty plays a leading part in the game of life.

Keep thy heart (or imagination) with all diligence, for out of it are the issues of life." (Prov. 4:23.)

This means that what man images, sooner or later externalizes in his affairs, I know of a man who feared a certain disease. It was a very rare disease and difficult to get, but he pictured it continually and read about it until it manifested in his body, and he died, the victim of distorted imagination.

So we see, to play successfully the game of life, we must train the imaging faculty. A person with an imaging faculty trained to image only good, brings into his life "every righteous desire of his heart" - health, wealth, love, friends, perfect self-expression, his highest ideals.

The imagination has been called, "The Scissors of The Mind," and it is ever cutting, cutting, day by day, the pictures man sees there, and sooner or later he meets his own creations in his outer world. To train the imagination successfully, man must understand the workings of his mind. The Greeks said: "Know Thyself."

There are three departments of the mind, the *subconscious, conscious and superconscious.* The subconscious, is simply power, without direction. It is like steam or electricity, and it does what it is directed to do; it has no power of induction.

Whatever man feels deeply or images clearly, is impressed upon the subconscious mind, and carried out in minutest detail.

For example: a woman I know, when a child, always "made believe" she was a widow. She "dressed up" in black clothes and wore a long black veil, and people thought she was very clever and amusing. She grew up and married a man with whom she was deeply in love. In a short time he died and she wore black and a sweeping veil for many years. The picture of herself as a widow was impressed upon the subconscious mind, and in due time worked itself out, regardless of the havoc created.

The conscious mind has been called mortal or carnal mind.

It is the human mind and sees life as it *appears to be.* It sees death, disaster, sickness, poverty and limitation of every kind, and it impresses the subconscious.

The superconscious mind is the God Mind within each man, and is the realm of perfect ideas.

In it, is the "perfect pattern" spoken of by Plato, *The Divine Design*; for there is a Divine Design for each person.

There is a place that you are to fill and no one else can fill, something you are to do, which no one else can do."

There is a perfect picture of this in the superconscious mind. It usually flashes across the conscious as an unattainable ideal - "something too good to be true."

In reality it is man's true destiny (or destination) flashed to him from the Infinite Intelligence which is *within himself.*

Many people, however, are in ignorance of their true destinies and are striving for things and situations which do not belong to them, and would only bring failure and dissatisfaction if attained.

For example: A woman came to me and asked me to "speak the word" that she would marry a certain man with whom she was very much in love. (She called him A. B.)

I replied that this would be a violation of spiritual law, but that I would speak the word for the right man, the "divine selection," the man who belonged to her by divine right.

I added, "If A. B. is the right man you can't lose him, and if he isn't, you will receive his equivalent." She saw A. B. frequently but no headway was made in their friendship. One evening she called, and said, "Do you know, for the last week, A. B. hasn't seemed so wonderful to me." I replied, "Maybe he is not the divine selection - another man may be the right one." Soon after that, she met another man who fell in love with her at once, and who said she was his ideal. In fact, he said all the things that she had always wished A. B. would say to her.

She remarked, "It was quite uncanny."

She soon returned his love, and lost all interest in A. B.

This shows the law of substitution. A right idea was substituted for a wrong one, therefore there was no loss or sacrifice involved.

Jesus Christ said, "Seek ye first the kingdom of God and his righteousness; and all these things shall be added unto you," and he said the Kingdom *was within man.*

Chapter 1 - The Game

The Kingdom is the realm of *right ideas*, or the divine pattern.

Jesus Christ taught that man's words played a leading part in the game of life. "By your words ye are justified and by your words ye are condemned."

Many people have brought disaster into their lives through idle words.

For example: A woman once asked me why her life was now one of poverty of limitation. Formerly she had a home, was surrounded by beautiful things and had often tired of the management of her home, and had said repeatedly, "I'm sick and tired of things - I wish I lived in a trunk," and she added: "Today I am living in that trunk." She had spoken herself into a trunk. The subconscious mind has no sense of humor and people often joke themselves into unhappy experiences.

For example: A woman who had a great deal of money, joked continually about "getting ready for the poorhouse."

In a few years she was almost destitute, having impressed the subconscious mind with a picture of lack and limitation.

Fortunately the law works both ways, and a situation of lack may be changed to one of plenty.

For example: A woman came to me one hot summer's day for a "treatment" for prosperity. She was worn out, dejected and discouraged. She said she possessed just eight dollars in the world. I said, "Good, we'll bless the eight dollars and multiply them as Jesus Christ multiplied the loaves and fishes," for He taught that every man had the power to bless and to multiply, to heal and to prosper.

She said, "What shall I do next?"

I replied, "Follow intuition. Have you a 'hunch' to do anything, or to go anywhere?" Intuition means, intuition, or to be taught from within. It is man's unerring guide, and I will deal more fully with its laws in a following chapter.

The woman replied: "I don't know - I seem to have a 'hunch' to go home; I've just enough money for carfare." Her home was in a distant city and was one of lack and limitation, and the reasoning mind (or intellect) would have said: "Stay in New York and get work and make some money." I replied, "Then go home - never violate a hunch." I spoke the following words for her: *Infinite Spirit open the way for great abundance for --. She is an irresistible magnet for all that belongs to her by divine right."* I told her to repeat it continually also. She left for home immediately. In calling on a woman one day, she linked up with an old friend of her family.

Through this friend, she received thousands of dollars in a most miraculous way. She has said to me often, "Tell people about the woman who came to you with eight dollars and a hunch."

There is always plenty on *man's pathway*; but it can only be *brought into manifestation* through desire, faith or the spoken word. Jesus Christ brought out clearly that man must make the first *move.*

Ask, and it shall be given you, seek, and ye shall find, knock, and it shall be opened unto you. (Mat. 7:7).

In the scriptures we read: Concerning the works of my hands, command ye me."

Infinite Intelligence, God, is ever ready to carry out man's smallest or greatest demands.

Every desire, uttered or unexpressed, is a demand. We are often startled by having a wish suddenly fulfilled.

For example: One Easter, having seen many beautiful rose-trees in the florists' windows, I wished I would receive one, and for an instant saw it mentally being carried in the door.

Easter came, and with it a beautiful rose-tree. I thanked my friend the following day, and told her it was just what I had wanted.

She replied, "I didn't send you a rose-tree, I sent you lilies!"

The man had mixed the order, and sent me a rose-tree simply because I had started the law in action, and *I had to have a rose-tree.*

Nothing stands between man and his highest ideals and every desire of his heart, but doubt and fear. When man can "wish without worrying," every desire will be instantly fulfilled.

I will explain more fully in a following chapter the scientific reason for this and fear must be erased from the consciousness. It is man's only enemy - fear of lack, fear of failure, fear of sickness, fear of loss and a feeling *of insecurity on some plane.* Jesus Christ said: "Why are ye fearful, oh ye of little faith?" (Mat. 8:26) So we can see we must substitute faith for fear, for fear is only inverted faith; it is faith in evil instead of good.

The object of the game of life is to see clearly one's good and to obliterate all mental pictures of evil. This must be done by impressing the subconscious mind with a realization of good. A very brilliant man, who has attained great success, told me he had suddenly erased all fear from his consciousness by reading a sign which hung in a room. He saw printed, in large letters this statement - *Why worry, it will probably never happen."* These words were stamped indelibly upon his subconscious mind, and he has now a firm conviction that only good can come into his life, therefore only *good can manifest.*

In the following chapter I will deal with the different methods of impressing the subconscious mind. It is man's faithful servant but one must be careful to give it the right orders. Man has ever a silent listener at his side – his subconscious mind.

Chapter 1 - The Game

Every thought, every word is impressed upon it and carried out in amazing detail. It is like a singer making a record on the sensitive disc of the phonographic plate. Every note and tone of the singer's voice is registered. If he coughs or hesitates, it is registered also. So let us break all the old bad records in the subconscious mind, the records of our lives which we do not wish to keep, and make new and beautiful ones.

Speak these words aloud, with power and conviction: "I now smash and demolish (by my spoken word) every untrue record in my subconscious mind. They shall return to the dust-heap of their native nothingness, for they came from my own vain imaginings. I now make my perfect records through the Christ within - The records of *Health, Wealth, Love and perfect self-Expression.*" This is the square of life, *The Game completed.*

In the following chapters, I will show how man can *change* his *conditions by changing his words.* Any man who does not know the power of the word, is behind the times.

Death and Life are in the power of the tongue." (Prov. 18:21.)

11

In this session:

- The Square of Life
- Thoughts are Energy
- The Three Levels of Consciousness of the Mind and Their Power
  * Subconscious * Conscious * Superconscious
- The Quiet Voice Within – Intuition – the God Part
- Man's Enemy is Within – FEAR
- Divine Life Path Versus Ignorance of True Destiny
- The Divine Selection/Divine Right
- Manifesting Abundance
- Re-Writing Our Subconscious Records/CD
- Infinite Intelligence – God is Ever Ready!
- Recap and Journal Pages

NOTE: Chapter One's workbook session is long and has a LOT of information. Please take your time and allow yourself to fully integrate all that is here before moving on to the next chapter and session.

We begin each session with a prayer and a few quiet moments to open our mind and heart to the limitless possibilities of God and of our individual spiritual being-ness. Breathe deeply and ask Archangel Michael to surround you with God's Divine White Light of Protection and set your intention to connect with your higher self – the God Part within.

Father, Mother, God, Creator of All That Is…

I claim my personal power and open the way to see clearly my field of potentiality, my field of infinite possibilities. I cut the ties of beliefs and thought patterns that no longer serve me in all directions of time thereby removing them from my consciousness, my subconscious and my superconscious. I fearlessly step into the magnificence of the true essence of who I am – One with God. I graciously accept all that is mine by divine right, under grace in a miraculous way and commit to fulfill all that I came to be, have and do in this incarnation on Mother Earth at this time.

Amen

Ask your guides, angels and teachers to be present with you to help you open your heart, mind and spirit to the infinite possibilities.

The inner workings of Chapter One, The Game, can be overwhelming… Take each section slowly – one at a time at your own pace.

> ***The object of the Game of Life is to see clearly one's good and to obliterate all mental pictures, thoughts and beliefs of negativity.***

THE SQUARE OF LIFE

Florence states that our square of life is:

- Health – A healthy physical body that houses our spirit
- Love - Relationships that are fulfilling and love based
- Perfect Self-Expression – Work that fulfills our passion that we love
- Wealth – Cash flow that fulfills our needs and desires

If we are truly in tune/connected with the God Part within us, there will be no fear or doubt in our lives. Our thoughts, feelings and actions are either love based or fear based – there is no in between. This is profound knowledge.

When we live from an absolute love based foundation, our thoughts will be "positive" and of our "highest good;" therefore, we are a magnet for the abundance we desire in the four areas of the square of life – true prosperity.

We will become magnets for what we continually focus on – love based thoughts, feelings and beliefs – magnetizing to us more of our highest good – based in love.

Receiving prosperous abundance is NOT a reward for good behavior. We live in an abundant universe. We choose with our thoughts and deep seated beliefs whether we are in abundance of lack or prosperity. Abundance from the Universe/God is our birthright.

When we choose to live our lives from a source of love, abundant in prosperity, we are open to freely share God's love from deep within promoting peace and joy throughout the world.

It is then that we reach an understanding of the "All" that God is and live our lives from a source of Love – not Fear. Living from the love source shifts us to a magnet for prosperous love, health, wealth and perfect self-expression. The square of Life fulfilled.

THOUGHTS ARE ENERGY

"Whatsoever a man soweth that shall he also reap." This is deeper than just a man's actions and words. This includes man's thoughts as well. Man's thoughts, actions and words are powerful. Whatever a man sends out in word, action or *thought*, will return to him – how can this be?

What we continually think about *will* manifest into our lives. If we continually focus on lack, we will always be in an abundant state of lack. If we focus, worry and fret over a specific disease or illness – our body will attract it. If we continually focus on how blessed and prosperous we are – we will be! If we could see the energy surrounding us that our words and thoughts create, we would be more careful, indeed, as to the type of energy – positive or negative, that we put out!

We in the 21st century understand that when we put something in the microwave and turn it on, it's going to get cooked and/or hot. We know this to be a fact, but it is hard for us to understand that our very thoughts also hold great energy – *that our minds are like a microwave creating energy not only within, but also sending that energy out into the world to manifest the reality of our lives.*

Our thoughts and words ARE energy that create our reality.

What does your square of life look like? Are all areas of your life working? If we honestly evaluate what we continually think of, will we be horrified? Yet, will we see a clear picture of how and why our reality is what it is?

What we continually think about *WILL* materialize in our lives!

What we believe deep within us *WILL* manifest in our lives!

Florence uses the example of a man who feared a certain disease, continually thinking of it caused his energy (his fear), to make him a magnet for the disease, thereby, bringing it into his reality.

She states to "play successfully the game of life" (bring what we really want into our lives), "we must train the imaging faculty." The imaging faculty is our mind – monitoring our thoughts is how to train our mind.

Training our mind to bring good into our lives typically doesn't happen on its own. Beginning as babies, we are physically conditioned to fear and limit ourselves. By the time we become teenagers we have developed limiting thought patterns and beliefs. Most of our lives are lived believing in lack, fear and personal limitations.

The Game of Life states: "Jesus Christ taught that man's words play a leading part in the game of life. 'By your words ye are justified and by your words ye are condemned.'" The three levels of consciousness will help us to understand this.

THE THREE LEVELS OF CONSCIOUSNESS OF THE MIND AND THEIR POWER:

The true POWER of our mind is governed by the three levels of consciousness:

1) subconscious
2) conscious
3) superconscious

SUBCONSCIOUS

The **subconscious** mind is our soul – our spirit. It is like a record or CD. We imprint on it the things we have deep seated feelings of or what we repeatedly think of – PLUS the subconscious mind holds the experiences of past lives.

Unfortunately it is the part of the mind with the least supervision – sometimes we become magnets for negative things and we aren't even aware that we have deep seated feelings that are negative. Example: if we have a fear of lack – it lives eternally in the subconscious mind making us a magnet for lack. Of course, the flip side of negative is positive. So if we have deep seated feelings that are positive, such as completely believing we are worthy to receive our highest good – that we are <u>naturally prosperous</u> - then we become a magnet for prosperity. Unfortunately the physical world rarely conditions us in such a positive way.

The subconscious mind works with the superconscious/the universe to match the vibrational frequency/energy of what we continually focus on to us. Our vibrational frequency attracts people and things of the same vibrational frequency – this is the Law of Attraction.

The Superconscious holds our Field of Potentiality. The Universe is virtually a limitless supply warehouse with more than enough for everyone. There is no lack – only prosperity.

We also must keep in mind that the subconscious mind has NO sense of humor – our conscious mind creates the energy and our subconscious mind/the Universe works together to create what we've "wished" for, continually think about or have deep seated feelings of.

Florence used the example of the woman who repeatedly said she was getting ready for the poorhouse. The woman was joking, but she became almost destitute. Her words created the energy of lack and limitation and her subconscious mind worked behind the scenes and brought it into her reality.

Another example is of the young woman who "made believe" that she was a "widow" as a child. Her continual "pretending" that she was a widow, brought being a widow into her reality as an adult. Her *subconscious mind* – harboring her deep seated belief – her energy filled thoughts – manifested such a situation.

If the deep seated belief is negative – it is up to us to first determine that we are experiencing it, then, take the necessary steps to dissipate – completely eliminate – the negative feelings. Discerning the negative deep seated belief is the key. Often times this negative feeling, such as unworthiness, stems from the core of our being (perhaps even from a previous life).

WORKBOOK ITEM ONE:

Let's explore what your deep seated beliefs are with regard to fear of lack and feelings of worthiness.

Sit quietly and think about your square of life. Think about it honestly. Do you have any deep seated negative beliefs about yourself? Are you engulfed with fear of lack? When you think about being worthy to receive good things in your life, where do you feel it in your body and what do you feel? Do you feel warm and fuzzy, elated and joyful or do you feel like perhaps you don't deserve good things?

Read each section of the square of life and evaluate how you feel when you digest the words. Identify your feelings of worthiness or unworthiness. As you read each section do you truly feel deep within you that you are worthy to receive the abundance of the section? Write your answers in the section – be completely honest and truthful!

My Square of Life Form – Identifying My Beliefs

Health – A healthy physical body that houses my spirit
Love - Relationships that are fulfilling and love based
Perfect Self-Expression – Work that fulfills my passion that I love
Wealth – Cash flow that fulfills my needs and desires

Did you find yourself experiencing feelings of unworthiness? If you did not, congratulations! Good things in your life are *not rewards for good behavior* – each one of us is a profoundly loved child of God. It is our birthright to receive good things – Prosperous Abundance in the Square of Life. God, Infinite Spirit, The Creator, Our Heavenly Father, is a loving being who has great abundance for each one of us, it is up to us to use our free will wisely and allow ourselves to receive the prosperous abundance.

Feeling worthy to receive prosperous abundance, our birthright is a challenge for most of us. Through physical world conditioning we feel limited in what we can receive – limited in what we can do – limited in what we can be. Know that in God, there are no limits.

Use the Journal Page to write about what you have discovered. Were you surprised at what you learned about the inner workings of your subconscious thoughts?

JOURNAL PAGE:

WORKBOOK ITEM TWO:

This exercise is designed to help you identify more specifically your true feelings of worthiness to receive the prosperous abundance God has for you. You will identify negative feelings, thought patterns and beliefs and rid yourself of them.

Read the heading of each section of the Square of Life Form. Evaluate where you feel an emotion in your body. Identify what the emotion is – joy, happiness, elation, worry, anxiety, fear, etc. Write down a one word summary of the emotion (anger, joy, happiness, fear) under each section. Then review each section honestly and write down what you feel would make each area better.

Square of Life Form – Identifying Emotions/Feelings

My Health	My Love	My Wealth	My Work

Use the Journal Page to write about what you discovered about your feelings of being worthy. Look back at your life – do you see times when you "thought" yourself worthy, then at the last moment became fearful that you weren't – you blocked your highest good from coming to you – didn't you?

Sometimes we are self saboteurs. We all do it on occasion, but we have the power to get rid of fear and doubt and allow ourselves to receive God's abundance – all that is ours by divine right!

JOURNAL PAGE:

WORKBOOK ITEM THREE:

Two methods are offered to release deep seated negative beliefs and thought patterns identified in the previous workbook item: The Sedona Method® of Release (a releasing technique) and the Healing Circle of Love (a guided meditation). You may choose which one resonates with you:

The Sedona Method® of Release

This procedure is shockingly simple and extremely powerful! It is based upon The Sedona Method® releasing technique, a simple way to let go of any negative thoughts, feelings or emotions that may arise and is printed with permission of Sedona Training Associates, Sedona.com. The procedure will release completely negative beliefs and/or thought patterns that are blocking your receipt of prosperous abundance. *Refer to page 277 to use this procedure.*

Healing Circle of Love as given by Princess Diana and Mother Teresa

This powerful guided meditation shifts one from deep within to a source of love and works with relationships and life situations/events. *Refer to page 279 to use this procedure.*

Move through each section of the square of life releasing negative feelings with The Sedona Method® of Release or The Healing Circle of Love – or both! Use the Journal Page to write about the negative belief or thought pattern and your experience in releasing them.

JOURNAL PAGE:

CONSCIOUS

The **conscious** mind is the mind of the physical world – the one we work with every day. This part of us sees and takes in all that goes on around us. What we take into our minds is fed to our subconscious, such as negative news, negative movies, gossip, fear, and hatred – all negative things. Positive things that we take in are also initiated into the subconscious, such as love and joy

What does your conscious/subconscious diet consist of?

If you live your life on a diet of negativity, it must be stopped to open the doors to the abundance you seek. A diet of negativity forces us to live our lives from a source of fear. To remove negativity from our lives allows us to live our lives from a source of love. If negativity is in our lives, it is impossible to be love based. Set forth the intention of deleting the following negative energies from your life:

Gossip	Resentment	Complaining
Criticism of others	Sarcasm	Unforgiveness
Criticism of yourself	Anger	Judgment of yourself
Judgment of others	Hostility	Negativity of any kind…

Know this: Every thing we do, say or think is either love or fear base . There is no in between.
You may read more about the "Negativity Diet" in the book *The Four Spiritual Laws of Prosperity"* by Edwene Gaines.

WORKBOOK ITEM FOUR:

For the next seven (7) days, beginning today, fill out the My Life – Negative or Positive form. Under positive influences for each day write down the positive things you participated in - such as smiling at someone, helping someone, reading positive information, complimenting someone sincerely, blessing someone or something, praying, etc. Under negative influences for each day write down the negative things you participated in - such as watching negative news, gossiping, snapping at or arguing with someone, feeling hatred or anger within toward someone or some thing. At the end of each day, review the magnitude of negative vs positive. Do you find your life consisting of negativity more than positivity? If your positive side is longer than your negative, you're ahead of the game – congratulations!

My Life – Negative or Positive Form

Positive Influences - Living from Love Source	Negative Influences - Living from Fear Source
Day 1	
Day 2	
Day 3	
Day 4	
Day 5	

Day 6	
Day 7	

Use the Journal Page to write about your discoveries concerning how positive and how negative you are. Are you seeing the negative manifest in your life from your thoughts? What can you do to become more positive? Do you see how the negative things are based in fear? How the positive are based in love?

JOURNAL PAGE:

JOURNAL PAGE Continued:

WORKBOOK ITEM FIVE:

Negative, fear based thoughts are what we think about most of the time – this is normal – it is a physical world conditioning. This exercise is designed to make the creation of positive, love based thoughts your normal daily thought pattern – to live from a point of love – eliminating fear and negativity from your life.

The goal is to make it through the day without thinking or saying negative things. Set the intent now to eliminate negativity from your life. Begin today by identifying negative thoughts and things you say. Note each time you have a negative thought and each time you say something negative. Write down under the word TODAY how many of these negative thoughts you put into the Universe.

Do this for the next 30 days.

Note: You cannot fail at this. Negative thoughts *are* going to come into your mind – you live in a physical world laced with negativity. Do NOT beat yourself up for negative thoughts – this only adds to the negativity – instead be elated and proud of yourself that you *noticed* negative thoughts. Before this, in all probability, negative thoughts where rampant in your brain. ***The key is to identify that it is happening and transmute that negative fear based thought to one that is loving and positive. You can do this!***

With diligence you will have fewer and fewer negative thoughts. You may find that you don't have much to say in the beginning – because you're eliminating negative speech as well. However, by the end of the 30 days, not only will you have eliminated fear based negative thought patterns and beliefs, you will have replaced them with love based positive thought patterns and beliefs. Remember all thoughts are either fear based or love based.

TODAY	2	3	4	5	6	7
8	9	10	11	12	13	14
15	16	17	18	19	20	21

22	23	24	25	26	27	28
29	30					

What you will discover is that as you created more love based thoughts and beliefs, the Universe began to "match" to you the higher frequency love based energies of people, situations and things.

The more you fill your life with love based thoughts, the more love based people, situations, events and material items the Universe will "match" to you. This is how the Universe works with you, with everyone, everywhere, all the time. This is the Law of Attraction.

Remember, even though the physical world conditioning has taught you that fear and negativity is the way life is and they are forever to be the basis of your life – it isn't true. You have the choice to choose whether your continual line of thinking and believing is based on fear and lack or love and prosperity. You have the choice as to whether your frequency is tuned into the prosperity channel or the living with fear and lack channel.

You have the choice.

Use the Journal Pages to write about the exercise before you begin, then journal daily your experiences. You will see and experience more abundance in your life as you eliminate negativity and live from a love based foundation!

JOURNAL PAGE:

SUPERCONSCIOUS

The **superconscious** mind is the God Part of us - it harbors the abundance that God has for us and is most often blocked by the physical world conditioning of the conscious mind. The superconscious mind is the Universal Supply Warehouse, the All, Infinite Intelligence and Wisdom holding the answers of the universe. We can tap into this wisdom, this "still small voice within" through setting the intention to connect, believing we can connect and accepting the connection without fear through prayer, meditation and/or automatic dictation.

In opening our minds to understand, work with, and allow God to be an essential part of our lives, we elevate our consciousness to the possibility of the fourth dimensional realm – the limitlessness of Divine Mind – the love and oneness of God with All That Is. Florence opens that door in her teachings of *The Game of Life*. The exercises will help you to look through that door, to fearlessly step through and become One with God as the limitless spiritual being that you are!

It is here, in the superconscious mind, that we will "Remember" who we are. This is critical to our spiritual growth.

THE QUIET VOICE WITHIN – INTUITION – THE GOD PART

Florence states that "Jesus Christ said the Kingdom of God is *within* man."

What will we find when "looking within" to the superconscious part of us?

Living inside each human being – each and every one, is a God Part. God lives *within* each and every one of us. In the Divine Mind, man works in conjunction with God through the conscious, the subconscious and the superconscious. Due to physical world conditioning of fear, limiting thoughts and beliefs as well as profound feelings of unworthiness we tend to block the superconscious – our connection with the God Part within. It is time to dissipate the blocks and discover your true divine life path – a fulfilled square of life, prosperously abundant in health, love, finances and perfect self-expression.

Allowing yourself to receive the prosperous abundance God has for you is not greedy, nor selfish. If we as humans are NOT worrying about our love life, our health, our finances or our job, we are peaceful and fulfilled within - free to help others and spread joy and love throughout the world.

How do we tap this information? By looking within. By Looking Within we will discover our true connection with God. It won't be a "what if?" any longer – we will truly *know* it, *believe* it, *accept* it and no longer fear it!

How does one "look within?"

WORKBOOK ITEM SIX:

Looking within

Looking within requires patience, dedication and work. Find a quiet place. Sit quietly and breathe deeply. We're going to set the intention to meditate and connect with your higher self. Some will say they find it impossible to meditate because they can't quiet their mind (this is a negative statement) – others will fall asleep. This is of no consequence. The intention will be set.

There are many who share their method of meditation – it is up to you to find what works for you. Included here is meditation information from the angels.

Note: Burning Nag Champa incense will remind your senses of the meditative experience and move you along to achieve it when you smell it. Lowering the lights and using a burning candle or a battery operated one (for those of us who fall asleep) will also alert your senses to the meditative state. With patience you will determine what works best for you.

Setting the Intent: In prayer, ask Archangel Michael (or your favorite connection) to surround you with God's Divine White Light of protection and ask that only Spirits of God be allowed to communicate with you.

Sit quietly and ask your angels and guides to help you to look within and connect with your higher self – to experience your God Part. The more you set this intent and practice it, the more you will see, hear and know of your divine life path – the more you will understand the true, profound love that you and God are.

Read the entire exercise before you begin.

The Meditative State:

A Message from the Angels:

Breathe deeply and slowly – focus on your breathing – for it is through your breath that we are able to communicate most clearly with you. Breathe DEEPLY and fully. This is how you look within – to the God Part within you to tap into the answers of your heart – and they are all there – all the answers to the questions of your mind.

As you focus on your breathing, allow your questions to filter through – start with something easy, like the questions you have about nature and why nature is as it is. This way you don't have emotional feelings toward the answers – they are just answers. Allow them to come to you – this is practice for the personal questions about yourself, your purpose and your joy. The more you trust, the more freely the answers will make sense to you – the knowing, the hearing, the seeing of what we have to show you – ALLOW the images to flutter through your mind's eye. ALLOW – ALLOW – ALLOW!

It is easy to say, it is your imagination. But what is imagination? You are a masterly loved child of God who is surrounded in any given moment of the day by many, many angels, teachers and guides – all of whom wish to help you in every little thing that you do. Our greatest joy is to fulfill your requests – to help YOU to evolve and grow.

The love of God pulses through you, dear child – allow this love to touch others with your loving light. Joy is within you – allow it to be – it will touch others and bless you in ways that will surprise you. Acts of kindness are loving acts of God given to others for the joy of giving. Know, dear, sweet child, that you cannot "out give" God.

Sit in nature, dear, sweet child – allow yourself to see God in all that is around you – for in allowing, you will have the "eyes to see." Rejoice in this sight and be grateful for the blessing – it is then that you will begin to discover the true joy of Trust Within. The purpose of your life will unfold as if miraculously for you will truly become a miracle magnet for God's gifts of love. Allowing yourself to receive God's gifts is not selfish, for then you will have more and more to share with others. Your gifts will come in all ways - allow yourself to receive, dear child.

Know that as a child of God it is your birthright to receive all that God has for you – look within, dear child as we have explained and allow yourself to experience the true joy of God.

Your loving angels… "For within you, I live…" Jesus…

The Meditative Journey – *Sacred Space ~ Build It and They Will Come:* Allow yourself to relax and experience the sharing of God. Take in what you see, what you hear, and what comes forward from within you as "knowing." Ask questions to clarify anything you are unsure of. ***Refer to page 283 to use this meditation.***

Many who complain of mind chatter and not being able to connect, are connecting and don't realize it! The pictures, thoughts, movies and knowing that they see, hear and know is the angelic realm!

Look *honestly* at the ins and outs of your life – your personality, your motives, how you treat people, how you treat yourself, how you honor God – do you treat others with honor and respect? Do you treat yourself with honor and respect? Do you live your life from a point of love? Or fear? Are you fear based? Are you selfish? Are you judgmental? Do you touch others from your heart? Or do you ignore them? Do you use your free will wisely and allow yourself to connect with God and ask for His guidance, His wisdom? And do you allow Him to work in your life? Or are you just lip service?

Gratitude and Journaling: When you are finished, return to the physical world and thank your guides, angels and teachers for their help in making your connection.

Use the Journal Page to write about what you have discovered.

JOURNAL PAGE:

WORKBOOK ITEM SEVEN:

Tapping into the Quiet Voice Within – Your Intuition – Your God Part

Recognizing and truly listening to the God Part within us takes practice and patience and is completely possible! Once we identify the part of our body that gives us the "yes" or "no" answer all we have to do is allow it to be and use it.

To Begin the Process of Recognition: In prayer, ask Archangel Michael (or your favorite connection) to surround you with God's Divine White Light of protection. Sit quietly and ask your angels and guides to help you to connect with your higher self – to experience your God Part. The more you set this intent and practice it, the easier it will be to understand the "yes" and "no" answers God will give you.

Allow yourself to relax and experience the sharing of God.

To Define the "Yes" and the "No" Answers: Ask a question that you know the answer is "yes." If the sky is blue and cloudless outside, ask, "Is the sky blue and cloudless outside?" If it is night time, adjust the question accordingly. Acknowledge where you feel the answer and notice HOW the "YES" answer feels.

Then, ask a question that you *know* the answer is "no." Acknowledge where you feel the answer and notice HOW the "NO" answer feels.

Repeat the above using different questions until you recognize easily the feelings that are generated by the "yes" and the "no" answers.

Use the Journal Page to write about what you have discovered.

To learn more about the God Part within, you may refer to the book: "A *Still, Small Voice*" by Echo Bodine.

JOURNAL PAGE:

WORKBOOK ITEM EIGHT:

To experience Automatic Dictation from the Angelic Realm of God it is not necessary to enter a spiritual state such as meditation. You may hand write your messages or type them on a computer or typewriter.

Setting the Intent: In prayer, ask Archangel Michael (or your favorite connection) to surround you with God's Divine White Light of protection and ask that only Spirits of God be allowed to communicate with you.

Sit quietly and ask your angels and guides to help you to look within and connect with your higher self – to experience your God Part. The more you set this intent and practice it, the more you will see, hear and know of your divine life path – the more you will understand the true, profound love that God has for you.

Automatic Dictation: Ask a question or begin to write/type your own thoughts – often times the angels will interrupt your thought flow with the answer and/or their message. You will receive their information as words, pictures, movie, or perhaps a knowing within. Write/type everything you get – even if it makes no sense to you at the time – just allow the information to come. With practice, patience and trust, you will be receiving clear, accurate messages!

To the conditioned human brain, this sounds too easy to be true. Let go of the physical world conditioning that talking to God isn't possible and allow your connection to BE!

Message from the angels: "We come to you as a whisper. Soft and gentle. It will seem as your own thoughts, but we will stop and start. If you hear three words, type or write the three words. There may be a pause before the next words, but they will come. Do not force it, us or you."

Angelspeake How to Talk With Your Angels by Barbara Mark and Trudy Griswold

For more information on Automatic Dictation with the Angelic Realm, please pick up a copy of *"Angelspeake How to Talk with Your Angels"* by Barbara Mark and Trudy Griswold.

Use the Journal Page to write about your experience and discoveries.

JOURNAL PAGE:

In God, all things are possible!

MAN'S ENEMY IS WITHIN - FEAR

Florence states that man's only enemy is fear – fear of lack, fear of failure, fear of sickness, fear of loss. Fear is a physical world conditioning. As babies we do not come into this world with fear in our hearts – it is a learned response and becomes a *normal* part of our lives - like breathing. Fear keeps us from joy, love, peace and happiness.

Conversations with God, by Neale Donald Walsch, tells us that man created his greatest enemy through doubt – "FEAR."

Fear is the nail that keeps the door of prosperous abundance nailed shut.

Jesus Christ said: "Why are ye fearful, oh ye of little faith?"

Everything we do, everything we say, everything we think, is either based in love or in fear. It is the enlightened who know that there is a choice – to fear, or not to fear. Some of us think we don't live with fear. Most of us don't recognize it as such. The first step to ridding ourselves of it is to identify it and discern where and why we feel it.

WORKBOOK ITEM NINE:

A. Sit quietly and think about the dreams you have had for the following items. Under each item write about your dreams.

Dream List Form

* things you would like to do	* what you could do for others

* positive changes around you in work	* your relationships

What has stopped you from doing the things listed in the exercise? Is fear a huge factor? What about limiting beliefs and thought patterns that are based in fear? Perhaps the negativity of others holds you back – what would they think?

What if you knew you couldn't fail – then what would you do? How creative would you be? How healthy? How much in love? How financially secure? How abundant in all things, would you be? Did you perhaps feel somewhat unworthy to realize your dream? As stated before, good things in your life are not rewards for good behavior – you are a profoundly loved child of God and it is your birthright to receive good things.

After reviewing how FEAR has held you captive, you now see you have a choice. You've identified that fear is a factor in your life. Do you choose to live with fear or do you choose to live without it in love?

Fear is tricky because you've lived with it for so long; it feels like it is a part of you. Fear disguises itself, hiding in your subconscious until you make the effort to identify it and be rid of it.

Think about the dreams that have eluded you. Use the Journal Page to write about them and your findings through this exercise.

JOURNAL PAGE:

JOURNAL PAGE continued:

B. Identify in your body where you feel the fear that held you back from fulfilling your dreams. Refer to The Sedona Method® of Release and/or The Healing Circle of Love. Use one or both of these procedures repeatedly until you no longer feel the fear sensations within that has prevented you from fulfilling your dreams.

Use the Journal Page to write about your experience in releasing the fear based feelings. Do you feel lighter and freer? You will begin to see changes as a result of the experience of releasing – some may be instantaneous! You are shifting from within and the without has no choice but to shift as well! In writing about all these things you will see your progression of enlightenment and growth.

JOURNAL PAGE:

DIVINE LIFE PATH VERSUS IGNORANCE OF TRUE DESTINY

Florence states that "many people are in ignorance of their true destinies and are striving for things and situations which do not belong to them, and would only bring failure and dissatisfaction if attained."

Each one of us has our own Field of Potentiality that consists of our Perfect Square of Life. Often times we see something (material or otherwise) that someone else has and we want it just because *they* have it – not because it is something we truly desire. This material item, relationships, etc. is in *their* Field of Potential – not ours. We are magnificent manifestors, therefore, when we focus our thoughts on attaining what they have, we manifest it into our lives and it brings failure and dissatisfaction to us.

Plus we are conditioned by the teachings of the physical world to live in fear. The act of living in fear makes us a magnet for unhappy, unhealthy situations, events and relationships.

As we live our lives in the physical world of earth, our spiritual selves are often times buried beneath the conditioning of fear based thoughts and beliefs. The more buried we become, the more lost and scattered we are – unsure of not only where we are going, our goals and our beliefs, but who we truly are.

We are gifted, profoundly loved children of God. Our Father, God, has great abundance for us if we can release all the physical world conditioning, fear and worry, to have TRUST and experience FAITH in Him.

In living in the physical world, most of us float through our lives, floundering around, trying to get a grip on goals, dreams, reality, fear, happiness. We live "unconsciously." *Just what are we really supposed to be doing?* We're scattered because we're *not connecting* with our higher selves – our God Part. It is imperative that we work in tandem with our God Part to discern and remember who we are.

Each one of us has a Divine Life Path – the path of spiritual enlightenment – of spiritual growth – the path to unconditional love – to become One with God. That is what we are all here to do – to rise to a level of consciousness that accepts and allows unconditional love.

How do we find our true Divine Life Path?

We look within – we connect with the God Part within and learn to trust, respect and honor it.

WORKBOOK ITEM TEN:

Use the *Sacred Space ~ Build It and They Will Come* meditation experience on page 283 to connect with God and ask Him to show you the plan for your gifts – ask Him to reveal to you – to bring forward, your heartfelt desires of life as a human on this planet. Ask Him to show you the place that only you can fill. Then *allow* Him to show you.

Allow yourself to relax and experience the sharing of God. Take in what you see, what you hear, and what comes forward from within you as "knowing." Ask questions to clarify anything you are unsure of.

When you are finished, return to the physical world and thank your guides, angels and teachers for their help in making your connection. Do not be discouraged if you "feel" like you didn't get anything. God, the angels, our guides and teachers communicate with us all the time, but we don't recognize them. We think it is our own mind chatter. Use the Journal Page to write about anything you get – it could be a symbol, a movie, pictures, a knowing within, or you may hear words. These are the communications of the angelic realm. With practice you will learn to discern them from the mind chatter.

The things you "get" may not even make sense today. Ask God to clarify – He will. You will be amazed at the "signs" that come to you to clarify your conversations/connections with God.

Repeat the connection/meditation exercise *Sacred Space ~ Build It and They Will Come* as often as you can.

JOURNAL PAGE:

THE DIVINE SELECTION/DIVINE RIGHT

Asking God to send to us the Divine Selection is allowing the Law of Substitution to bring to us our highest good. We are asking to receive what we want or its equivalent. Only God sees the bigger picture and knows what is in our best interest – our highest good. God has *only our best interest* at heart – He is never judgmental or punishing – we are the ones who judge and punish! We must see through the physical world limits and see ourselves as God does – beautiful rainbows of loving energy – an energy entity of Him.

In asking for the Divine Selection – what we want or its equivalent to come to us by Divine Right, we open the door to receive the very best God has for us.

To receive what is "best" for us we must learn to "ask aright." We must connect with God and imprint in our superconscious the trust in allowing God to provide for us what is best – what we desire or its equivalent. Everything we desire falls into one of the four categories of the Square of Life – health, wealth, love or perfect self-expression. God has prosperous abundance for each of us in all these areas – can we trust Him to provide it – to be our supply?

Example: the woman who was, in reality, in love with the wrong man. Florence asked God/The Universe for the right man – the "divine selection" – the man who belonged to her by divine right. In so doing, free will was used *wisely* to ask for that which was her highest good – hers by "divine right."

(Encarta Dictionary: di-vine right (noun) coming directly from God.)

The feelings the woman had for the "wrong" man dissipated and she grew to love the "right man." By ***trusting and having faith in God***, the woman opened the doors to receive what was hers by "divine right" - her highest good. Even though, originally she wanted another man, she practiced *Free Will, Trust and Faith* and received abundance in love – the "Divine Selection by Divine Right."

MANIFESTING ABUNDANCE

"Jesus Christ multiplied the loaves and the fishes. He taught that *every man* has the power to bless and to multiply, to heal and to prosper."

In digesting this statement we must strip away physical world conditioning to understand the simplicity of it: ***It is every human's birthright to have a fulfilled prosperous square of life – health, wealth, love and perfect self-expression, because all humans are profoundly loved children of God with*** *a God Part within. Having a God Part within gives each one of us the power to bless, to multiply, to heal and to prosper.*

"*Ask,* and it shall be given you, seek, and ye shall find, knock, and it shall be opened unto you. (Matthew 7:7)"

We live in an abundant Universe. It is an open, unlimited Supply Warehouse – overflowing with every thing we could ever desire. The Universal Supply Warehouse has more than enough for every human on the planet. The Universe identifies the vibrational energy of what our focus is and matches that vibrational energy to us. The energy of our thoughts and words may be fear based, so the universe matches to us more fear. Or we may choose to supervise our thoughts and words, making sure they are love based, thereby, the universe matches to us that of the love vibration.

Our thoughts and our words are energy - that which we ask for, that which we continually think of will manifest into our lives. It is up to us as to whether it is our highest good or idle words and thoughts leading to disaster.

Trust and Faith in God/the Universe as our supply in all things will bring us the prosperous abundance in all things that we desire. In looking within and finding that inner light of God within us, we find it easier to trust and practice active faith in God's abilities.

To achieve this level of consciousness, our subconscious must be in order.

REWRITING OUR SUBCONSCIOUS RECORDS/CD

Florence tells us that "every thought, every word is impressed" upon our subconscious and carried out in amazing detail. This is the Law of Attraction. Unfortunately the details in our subconscious have been unconsciously written through negative conditioning of the physical world – fear, lack, selfishness, jealously, resentment, etc. Our goal is to delete from our subconscious these records of negativity and rewrite them with love, grace and the complete faith and trust in the knowledge of the limitless possibilities of us as One with God.

The tools to do this are:

1. Looking within honestly and discovering our fears – especially the fears we hide from ourselves. Workbook Item Nine A.

2. Completely releasing the fears we discovered. Workbook Item Nine B.

3. Looking within honestly to connect with the God Part within us. Refer to Workbook Item Ten.

4. Completely and fully allow ourselves to experience faith and trust in God. Work with Him directly by asking Him and allowing Him to help us re-write our subconscious with endless, limitless possibilities of God.

WORKBOOK ITEM ELEVEN

In the form below, write your understandings and experiences of the four tools. As you work with these tools, you will see a change in the dynamics of each one. As you implement them into your life, your life will begin to change – almost instantaneously – you are already seeing this. This exercise refers back to Workbook Item Nine A and B.

Tools Form

1. Looking within honestly and discovering our fears – especially the fears we hide from ourselves. Workbook Item Nine A.
2. Completely releasing the fears we discovered. Workbook Item Nine B.

3. Looking within honestly to connect with the God Part within us. Workbook Item Ten.

4. Completely and fully allow ourselves to experience faith and trust in God. Work with Him directly by asking Him and allowing Him to help us re-write our subconscious with endless, limitless possibilities of God.

In completing this exercise, you've looked deeper within yourself. Use the Journal Page to write about these changes, the blessings that come to you and the truths discovered. If you discovered fear or unworthiness lingering, use the tools you've learned to dissipate the feelings.

JOURNAL PAGE:

INFINITE INTELLIGENCE – GOD IS EVER READY!

Florence states that "Infinite Intelligence, God, is ever ready to carry out man's smallest or greatest demands." It is our birthright – not selfishness or greed.

We do not come here to the physical world alone. At any given moment of any given day we are a crowd of angels, guides and teachers as well as deceased loved ones. We come here with this entourage to help us achieve the spiritual growth we desire. We're very brave before we come back here – choosing many challenges that will ultimately lead us to an understanding of the Fourth Dimensional Realm of all encompassing, unconditional love.

Some religions teach us that we cannot talk to God directly. This simply is NOT true. We can communicate directly with God to ask for help or just to chat. God, His messengers, the angels, as well as our guides and teachers are with us every moment to help us experience our divine life path. They diligently work behind the scenes to help us without interfering in our free will. In order to receive more of their help, all we have to do is *implement our free will and ask*.

Ask God to make your life easier. He will.

RECAP

The first chapter, The Game, almost overloads us with information. Our eyes are opened to the realization that our words, actions and even our thoughts are very real, very powerful energy. We've discovered that there are deep seated beliefs – some we aren't even aware of having – some possibly coming from a past life, that create our reality.

We've learned of the workings of the three levels of consciousness and the tools to work with God instead of floundering on our own. In explaining the levels of consciousness, Florence gives us insight into connecting to the God Part within.

Now we have a clearer picture of the profound limited-ness of physical world conditioning and teachings. Fearlessly we face these fears we have been conditioned to by the physical world – identifying them and learning tools to eradicate them from our lives forever – leaving us free to graciously accept the prosperous abundance God has for us.

We are grasping the essence of the three levels of consciousness and the truly limitless spiritual being that humans are. We've learned blessed connection tools to access and pull forth that which is in our Field of Potentiality.

Allow yourself the time it takes to absorb and digest all the information.

The Game of Life is filled with repetition. This is how we learn. Each time we return to a subject throughout the book, we will have acquired a higher level of consciousness. Each time the workbook is opened a new level of understanding will be found – a new level of consciousness will be introduced and experienced. Ask God for clear understanding and guidance, He will help you.

You are making blessed changes in your thought patterns of the conscious, subconscious and superconscious. You are understanding spiritual law and you cannot go back. Move forward fearlessly and allow God's miraculous abundance to manifest in your life!

Honor yourself with time for you and God. Practice looking within, practice connecting with God. Be sure to thank your guides, teachers and angels for being in attendance and helping you to understand clearly.

Use the Journal Pages to look within, sit quietly and ponder. Reflect on what resonates deeply within you. Use automatic dictation and ask the angels and God any questions you have and allow them to give you the information.

What have you learned about the fear that resides within you?

JOURNAL PAGES:

JOURNAL PAGES continued:

"Yea, the Almighty shall be thy defense and thou shalt have plenty of silver."

One of the greatest messages given to the race through the scriptures is that God is man's supply and that man can release, *through his spoken word,* all that belongs to him by divine right. He must, however, have *perfect faith in his spoken word.*

Isaiah said, "My word shall not return unto me void, but shall accomplish that where it is sent." We know now, that words and thoughts are a tremendous vibratory force, ever molding man's body and affairs.

A woman came to me in great distress and said she was to be sued on the fifteenth of the month for three thousand dollars. She knew no way of getting the money and was in despair.

I told her God was her supply, and *that there is a supply for every demand.*

So I spoke the word! I gave thanks that the woman would receive three thousand dollars at the right time in the right way. I told her she must have perfect faith, and act her *perfect faith.* The fifteenth came but no money had materialized.

She called me on the 'phone and asked what she was to do.

I replied, "It is Saturday, so they won't sue you today, Your part is to act rich, thereby showing perfect faith that you will receive it by Monday." She asked me to lunch with her to keep up her courage. When I joined her at a restaurant, I said, "This is no time to economize. Order an expensive luncheon, act as if you have already received the three thousand dollars."

"All things whatsoever ye ask in prayer, *believing,* ye shall receive." "You must act as if you *had already received."* The next morning she called me on the 'phone and asked me to stay with her during the day, I said "No, you are divinely protected and God is never too late."

In the evening she 'phoned again, greatly excited and said, "My dear, a miracle has happened! I was sitting in my room this morning, when the doorbell rang, I said to the maid: 'Don't let anyone in.' The maid however, looked out the window and said, 'It's your cousin with the long white beard.'

So I said, 'Call him back. I would like to see him.' He was just turning the corner, when he heard the maid's voice, and he came back.

He talked for about an hour, and just as he was leaving he said, 'Oh, by the way, how are finances?'

I told him I needed the money, and he said, 'Why, my dear, I will give you three thousand dollars the first of the month.

I didn't like to tell him I was going to be sued. What shall I do? I won't receive it till the first of the month, and I must have it tomorrow." I said, "I'll keep on 'treating.'"

I said, "Spirit is never too late. I give thanks she has received the money on the invisible plane and that it manifests on time." The next morning her cousin called her up and said, "Come to my office this morning and I will give you the money." That afternoon, she had three thousand dollars to her credit in the bank, and wrote checks as rapidly as her excitement would permit.

If one asks for success and prepares for failure, he will get the situation he has prepared for. For example: A man came to me asking me to speak the word that a certain debt would be wiped out.

I found he spent his time planning what he would say to the man when he did not pay his bill, thereby neutralizing my words. He should have seen himself paying the debt.

We have a wonderful illustration of this in the bible, relating to the three kings who were in the desert, without water for their men and horses. They consulted the prophet Elisha, who gave them this astonishing message:

"Thus saith the Lord - Ye shall not see wind, neither shall ye see rain, yet make this valley full of ditches."

Man must prepare for the thing he has asked for, *when there isn't the slightest sign of it in sight.*

For example: A woman found it necessary to look for an apartment during the year when there was a great shortage of apartments in New York. It was considered almost an impossibility, and her friends were sorry for her and said, "Isn't it too bad, you'll have to store your furniture and live in a hotel." She replied, *"You needn't feel sorry for me, I'm a superman, and I'll get an apartment."*

She spoke the words: *"Infinite Spirit, open the way for the right apartment."* She knew there was a supply for every demand, and that she was "unconditioned," working on the spiritual plane, and that "one with God is a majority."

She had contemplated buying new blankets, when the "tempter," the adverse thought or reasoning mind, suggested, "Don't buy the blankets, perhaps, after all, you won't get an apartment and you will have no use for them." She promptly replied (to herself): "I'll dig my ditches by buying the blankets!" So she prepared for the apartment - acted as though she already had it.

She found one in a miraculous way, and it was given to her although there were over *two hundred other applicants.*

The blankets showed active faith.

It is needless to say that the ditches dug by the three kings in the desert were filled to overflowing. (Read, II Kings)

Getting into the spiritual swing of things is no easy matter for the average person. The adverse thoughts of doubt and fear surge from the subconscious. They are the "army of the aliens" which must be put to flight. This explains why it is so often, "darkest before the dawn."

A big demonstration is usually preceded by tormenting thoughts.

Having made a statement of high spiritual truth one challenges the old beliefs in the subconscious, and "error is exposed" to be put out.

This is the time when one must make his affirmations of truth repeatedly, and rejoice and give thanks that he has already received, "Before ye call I shall answer." This means that "every good and perfect gift" is already man's awaiting his recognition.

Man can only receive what he sees himself receiving.

The children of Israel were told that they could have all the land they could see. This is true of every man. He has only the land within his own mental vision. Every great work, every big accomplishment, has been brought into manifestation through holding to the vision, and often just before the big achievement, comes apparent failure and discouragement.

The children of Israel when they reached the "Promised Land," were afraid to go in, for they said it was filled with giants who made them feel like grasshoppers. "And there we saw the giants and we were in our own sight as grass-hoppers." This is almost every man's experience.

However, the one who knows spiritual law, is undisturbed by appearance, and rejoices while he is "yet in captivity." That is, he holds to his vision and gives thanks that the end is accomplished, he has received.

Jesus Christ gave a wonderful example of this. He said to his disciples: "Say not ye, there are yet four months and then cometh the harvest? Behold, I say unto you, lift up your eyes and look on the fields; for they are ripe already to harvest." His clear vision pierced the "world of matter" and he saw clearly the fourth dimensional world, things as they really are, perfect and complete in Divine Mind. So man must ever hold the vision of his journey's end and demand the manifestation of that which he has already received. It may be his perfect, health, love, supply, self-expression, home or friends.

They are all finished and perfect ideas registered in Divine Mind (man's own superconscious mind) and must come through him, not to him. For example: A man came to me asking for treatments for success. It was imperative that he raise, within a certain time, fifty-thousand dollars for his business. The time limit was almost up, when he came to me in despair. No one wanted to invest in his enterprise, and the bank had flatly refused a loan. I replied: "I suppose you lost your temper while at the bank, therefore your power. You can control any situation if you first control yourself." "Go back to the bank," I added, "and I will treat." My treatment was: "You are identified in love with the spirit of everyone connected with the bank. Let the divine idea come out of this situation." He replied, "Woman, you are talking about an impossibility. Tomorrow is Saturday; the bank closes at twelve, and my train won't get me there until ten, and the time limit is up tomorrow, and anyway they won't do it. It's too late." I replied, "God doesn't need any time and is never too late. With Him all things are possible." I added, "I don't know anything about business, but I know all about God." He replied: "It all sounds fine when I sit here listening to you, but when I go out it's terrible." He lived in a distant city, and I did not hear from him for a week, then came a letter. It read: "You were right. I raised the money, and will never again doubt the truth of all that you told me."

I saw him a few weeks later, and I said, "What happened? You evidently had plenty of time, after all." He replied, "My train was late, and I got there just fifteen minutes to twelve. I walked into the bank quietly and said, 'I have come for the loan,' and they gave it to me without a question."

It was the last fifteen minutes of the time allotted to him, and Infinite Spirit was not too late. In this instance the man could never have demonstrated alone. He needed someone to help him hold to the vision. This is what one man can do for another.

Jesus Christ knew the truth of this when he said: "If two of you shall agree on earth as touching anything that they shall ask, it shall be done for them of my Father which is in heaven." One gets too close to his own affairs and becomes doubtful and fearful.

The friend or "healer" sees clearly the success, health, or prosperity, and never wavers, because he is not close to the situation.

It is much easier to "demonstrate" for someone else than for one's self, so a person should not hesitate to ask for help, if he feels himself wavering.

A keen observer of life once said, "No man can fail, if some one person sees him successful." Such is the power of the vision, and many a great man owed his success to a wife, or sister, or a friend who "believed in him" and held without wavering to the perfect pattern!

Workbook Session Two - The Law of Prosperity

In this session:

- God is My Supply!
- Active Faith – Celebrating Receipt!
- God is Never Late
- Army of the Aliens
- Manifestation Comes *Through* Man – Not *To* Him
- The Power of Two
- Recap and Journal Pages

Begin this session by asking Archangel Michael to surround you with God's Divine White Light of Protection and set your intention to connect with your higher self – the God Part within.

Father, Mother, God, Creator of All That Is…

I claim my personal power and open the way to see clearly my field of potentiality, my field of infinite possibilities. I cut the ties of beliefs and thought patterns that no longer serve me in all directions of time thereby removing them from my consciousness, my subconscious and my superconscious. I fearlessly step into the magnificence of the true essence of who I am – One with God. I graciously accept all that is mine by divine right, under grace in a miraculous way and commit to fulfill all that I came to be, have and do in this incarnation on Mother Earth at this time.

Amen

Ask your guides, angels and teachers to be present with you to help you open your heart, mind and spirit to the infinite possibilities.

> **God is man's supply in all things. God does NOT need time**
> **and is NEVER late. Manifestation must come <u>through</u> man**
> **(by enlisting the superconscious mind – the God Part) not <u>to</u> him.**

GOD IS MY SUPPLY!

Florence states that "One of the greatest messages given to the race through the scriptures is that God is man's supply and that man can release, *through his spoken word,* all that belongs to him by divine right. He must, however, have *perfect faith in his spoken word."*

These words are profound within themselves. We can release the prosperous abundance God has for us through our words, thoughts and actions, but we can only receive it if we *have perfect faith in God as our supply – if we release our control of how we will receive!* This doesn't mean that we want to be or will be controlled. It means we allow God to be our partner and we work together as a team not only for our highest good – but also to fulfill the place that only we can fill in the physical world.

In the previous workbook session we talked about how good things that manifest into our lives are *not* rewards for good behavior. Each one of us is a profoundly loved child of God with a God Part residing within. God does not deny Himself, nor would He deny His beloved children. This is not easy for many of us to get our minds around. To do so, it is necessary to accept that God is a loving God – not judgmental and punishing. We would also need to accept that God loves us, truly loves *all* of us – each and every one. We must also accept that there is a part of God Himself *within* each one of us.

Note: Each one of us *does indeed* have a God Part within us, however, some of us have been known to suppress that part of us so far that the light is very hard to see – example: a mass murderer. The God Part is still there.

As we live our lives in the physical world of earth, our spiritual selves are often times buried beneath the conditioning of fear based thoughts and beliefs. The more buried we become, the more lost and scattered we are – unsure of not only where we are going, our goals and our beliefs, but *who* we truly are.

Our Father, Mother, God, has a fulfilled square of life for us if we can release all the physical world conditioning, fear and worry, and in its place practice TRUST and experience FAITH in Him.

Most of us feel lost and scattered – we don't know who we are because all three levels of consciousness are working independently of one another – scattered – instead of as a team – as One – with God. In connecting to the God Part within us, we experience the peace and fulfillment of connecting the three levels of consciousness – we "discover" who we are!

We are gifted, profoundly loved children of God.

God has great abundance for each one of us – it is up to us as to whether we choose to allow ourselves to be One with God in *active faith and trust believing from deep within that we are in receipt of all that we desire from our Field of Potentiality.*

WORKBOOK ITEM ONE:

This exercise is to clarify your thinking – it will eliminate a form of physical world conditioning. Under the ***God is My Supply*** column, take three to five minutes and write down all the things that God is the supply of. Then without stopping – go to the next column, ***God is NOT My Supply*** and write down all the things that God is not the supply of.

God is My Supply Form

God is My Supply:
God is NOT My Supply:

When you are finished, review the columns – is anything written in the ***God is NOT My Supply*** column? If there is, read through each item and carefully evaluate why you think God does <u>not</u> supply the item. Is it in the correct column? You will discover that the ***God is NOT My Supply*** column should be empty.

This exercise clearly defines how limitless God truly is, by consciously showing you that He is your supply in all things.

Use the Journal Page to write about your experience in discerning the basis of your supply. Don't skip the journaling!

JOURNAL PAGE:

ACTIVE FAITH – CELEBRATING RECEIPT!

Florence shares with us the example of the woman who needed $3,000 right away. Florence *spoke the word* and gave thanks that the woman would receive the money at the right time in the right way. Florence told the woman to have perfect faith and to act the *perfect faith*. They anchored the perfect faith by celebrating receipt by ordering an expensive lunch.

All three departments of the mind were employed. The Conscious mind activated the receipt of the money by *speaking the word – giving thanks for receipt.*

The Subconscious mind *recorded* she would receive the money through repetition of giving thanks - belief.

The Superconscious mind *trusted and practiced perfect faith* that God, indeed, was her supply by acknowledging the **sincerity** of her thanking God for receipt. At this point, the subconscious and superconscious believed she was in receipt – even though she had not.

By activating all three departments of the mind together as a team, the woman effectively paved the way to manifest the money into her reality. She raised her vibrational frequency of energy and she became a magnet for the vibrational frequency of the debt paid in full thereby, she received the money. She was based in love – no fear, no doubts – no blocks.

Florence states that "If one asks for success and prepares for failure, he will get the situation he has prepared for." Clearly, preparing for failure blocks receipt. Preparing for failure enlists the Subconscious mind to manifest what it believes will happen - failure. Preparing for failure destroys the faith and trust in God as the supply and splits the levels of consciousness to yet again work independently of one another.

Preparing for failure lowers the vibrational level of energy to that of failure; therefore, failure is what is attracted.

Preparing for success brings to full attention *active faith and trust* in God. Celebrating receipt of what we have asked for when there is no sign of it in site activates true *faith and trust*, and aligns our vibrational frequency of energy to that of which we desire – we become a magnet for it!

A simple example of active faith is what we do when we go to a restaurant. We order our food, and have faith and trust that the cook will fulfill our order. We prepare for receipt of the meal.

When we look at active faith in this way, it sounds easy.

WORKBOOK ITEM TWO:

Writing your Subconscious CD:

This exercise is designed to help us develop our visualization skills. Think of something you desire – something simple like a feather.

In choosing something we are not emotionally attached to, such as a feather, we do not give power to fear at the possibility of receipt.

Think of the feather – what color is it? What size is it? Are there any distinguishing marks on it? Is it soft or coarse? Visualize the feel of it in your hand.

We know that there isn't a feather in front of us, but we can visualize it and allow ourselves to believe it is there. In allowing yourself to experience the feelings of already having received the object, the emotions of receipt are activated – opulence is experienced!

Now visualize having already received the feather. Fill in the visualization column with what you are visualizing.

Write about how you achieved the feelings of receipt and what opulence feels like in the columns.

Note: You have no emotions of fear at not receiving the feather – you are non-resistant.

Writing the Subconscious CD Form

What I Desire	Visualization of Receipt	Receipt and Opulence

The purpose of this exercise is to achieve the feelings of Opulence, Wealth, and Affluence – to achieve it and know what it feels like. Then when practicing active faith, we will know the state of being that we are trying to achieve to write the record into our subconscious for manifestation.

Use the Journal Page to write about this experience. In the act of filling in the form and then writing about it in the journal, we anchor this process in the Subconscious – we explore the ins and outs of the process making it easier to implement into our lives.

If we go so far as to celebrate the feeling of opulence – the feeling of receipt – we further anchor and firmly set the record of receipt in our subconscious. It is then the *mission* of the subconscious/God/the Universal Supply Warehouse to match to our vibration the object of our desire for it has the same vibrational energy from the visualization of receipt. We become a magnet and the object of our desire becomes a magnet to us. The object of our desire then manifests into our life.

JOURNAL PAGE:

GOD IS NEVER LATE

Florence states that "Spirit is never too late." When we completely believe God to be our supply, our receipt has no other choice than to manifest in time. This belief elevates us to existing on the spiritual plane – as One with God/the Universe.

If we don't receive what we desire, we must evaluate our thoughts, words and actions. Did we negate receipt? This is explained in these words: "If one asks for success and prepares for failure, he will get the situation he has prepared for."

Florence's example of the man who spent his time planning what to do when he didn't get what he asked for shows us clearly how powerful our thoughts, actions and words are. The man magnetized to him failure.

With each experience of receiving God's best or the experience of *not* receiving, we must evaluate our thoughts, words and actions in regard to the situation. In evaluating the situation we step up to a new level of understanding – a higher consciousness when we look within to discern: WHY we received or WHY we didn't.

ARMY OF THE ALIENS

Florence states: "Getting into the spiritual swing of things is no easy matter for the average person. The adverse thoughts of doubt and fear surge from the subconscious. They are the "army of the aliens" which must be put to flight. This explains why it is so often, "darkest before the dawn."

In order to get into the spiritual swing of things, physical world conditioning of lack and limitation must be eradicated. Fear and worry are the "army of the aliens" and must be released. In today's physical world, we're conditioned to believe we're limited beings and we're all alone.

This is not true.

We are limitless spiritual beings.

We are a crowd of teachers, guides, angels and deceased loved ones in every moment of every day – we are, indeed, a crowd!

It would be easy to negate receipt by allowing seeming adversity to control our thoughts, thereby lowering our vibrational frequency. When *now* is the time to *bless* the adversity and claim the receipt of what we desire, Success!

In blessing adversity, it negates the negativity – blessing transmutes negativity to love – forcing the universe to "match" to us the vibration of the "love based blessing."

Bless the "Darkness before the Dawn."

WORKBOOK ITEM THREE:

You've done this exercise before, but you've learned a lot since then. Read the heading of each section of the Square of Life Form. Do you feel limitless as you ponder each column? Is your life full of possibilities? Honestly evaluate the status of the full square of your life. Where do you feel limited? Do you know why? Identify the feelings in the appropriate column.

If you feel limitless in any area, you feel elated – can you reach the level of opulence within?

Square of Life Form

My Health	My Love	My Wealth	My Work

Do you have an area that you know deep within that you are limitless? Look within and journal about this. In anchoring this information in your journal, you will have a reference point to look back on for help.

If you discover fear, limitedness, chaos, or confusion in any area of your square, return to The Sedona Method® of Release or the Healing Circle of Love to dissipate these feelings. Use the Journal Page to write about the experience of the evaluation and identification of limitlessness.

JOURNAL PAGE:

MANIFESTATION COMES *THROUGH* MAN – NOT *TO* HIM

Most religions teach us that God helps those who help themselves. An interpretation of this is that God helps those when they are wise enough to ask God for help. However, the true meaning of this goes deeper to the God Part within.

By tapping into the God Part within to receive what we've asked for, all receipt comes *through man – not to him.*

When we courageously integrate the three levels of consciousness, we become a magnet for what we desire; therefore; our good comes through our God Part to manifest in our lives. It isn't just *given to* us, but springs forth from within us.

By working with God, man is empowered from within to manifest the abundance that IS God. Remember, abundance comes in all areas of the square of life:

- Health – A healthy physical body that houses our spirit
- Love - Relationships that are fulfilling and love based
- Perfect Self-Expression – Work that fulfills our passion that we love
- Wealth – Cash flow that fulfills our needs and desires

We've practiced recognizing God within us. Truly connect with God and work with Him. Negate the physical world teachings that you are limited.

WORKBOOK ITEM FOUR:

Connecting with God through meditation reduces stress levels. The mind, body and spirit learn how to work together. Use this exercise as much as you possibly can.

Refer to the meditation Sacred Space ~ Build It and They Will Come. Connect with your God Part within to access what is now revealed to you at this higher state of being that you have achieved.

Allow yourself to relax and experience the sharing of God. Take in what you see, what you hear, and what comes forward from within you as "knowing." Ask questions to clarify anything you are unsure of.

Look within to discern how God brings prosperity through you – through your limitlessness. Do you see where you have blocked prosperity in the past? Are you seeing ways to release limiting thought patterns and beliefs and allow the limitlessness of your spiritual self to come forward and be who you truly are – a limitless child of God?

Use Automatic Dictation: Ask a question or begin to write/type your own thoughts – often times the angels will interrupt your thought flow with the answer and/or their message. You will receive their information as words, pictures, movie, or perhaps a knowing within. Write/type everything you get – even if it makes no sense to you at the time – just allow the information to come.

Ask God about your limitlessness. Allow yourself to be open to the answer!

When you are finished, return to the physical world and thank your guides, angels and teachers for their help in making your connection. Use the Journal Page to write about what you have discovered.

JOURNAL PAGE:

THE POWER OF TWO

Jesus said: "If two of you shall agree on earth as touching anything that they shall ask, it shall be done for them of my Father which is in heaven." Florence explained this clearly that "no man can fail, if some one person sees him successful. ...many a great man has owed his success to a wife, or sister, or a friend who believed in him and held without wavering to the perfect pattern!"

When two people raise their level of consciousness to hold without wavering their belief of receipt it must manifest. This is spiritual law. If one should begin to waver, the other is there for support.

Florence also shares with us how it is easier to see clearly the success, health or prosperity of another – this is because we are dissociated from the emotional side of the situation. Therefore, if you have no one in physical form to help you hold to your vision – to support you from wavering, step outside your situation and evaluate it as an unbiased third party who knows of God's limitless power to supply the abundance of your desires. Hold fast to the knowledge, to the Universal Truth, that *in God all things are possible.* By stepping outside the situation, you remove the limits and allow for the limitless possibilities – you can achieve the feeling of receipt and will be able to celebrate it showing active faith, thereby, anchoring faith and trust.

RECAP

The second chapter, The Law of Prosperity, brings to light yet more information of how to integrate the three levels of consciousness. When integration is achieved, we live our lives from the palm of God.

We work in conjunction with God. We freely use our free will to live from a source of love, thereby, raising our vibrational frequency to that of love to become a magnet for more love – our flow of the abundance we desire is energized!

Use the opportunity of the next few days to practice the tools of integration. Ask God questions, allow yourself to receive the answers. Practice will make working *with* God as easy and familiar as breathing…

Honor yourself and God in all that you do – allow yourself to be One with God – it is a choice. Monitor your thoughts, words and actions – are they love based or fear based?

Write in your journal the happy surprises that bless your life – for now you are consciously opening the door to receive that which you desire! God is lighting your Divine Life Path with the glow of His love and wisdom. YOU now have the eyes to see and experience all the miracles He has for you!

Be sure to thank your guides, teachers and angels for being in attendance and helping you to clearly understand God's work.

May you be profoundly blessed in this moment and in every moment after…

JOURNAL PAGES:

JOURNAL PAGES continued:

"By thy words thou shalt be justified, and by thy words thou shalt be condemned."

A person knowing the power of the word, becomes very careful of his conversation. He has only to watch the reaction of his words to know that they do "not return void." Through his spoken word, man is continually making laws for himself.

I knew a man who said, "I always miss a car. It invariably pulls out just as I arrive."

His daughter said: "I always catch a car. It's sure to come just as I get there." This occurred for years. Each had made a separate law for himself, one of failure, one of success. This is the psychology of superstitions.

The horse-shoe or rabbit's foot contains no power, but man's spoken word and belief that it will bring good luck creates expectancy in the subconscious mind, and attracts a "lucky situation." I find however, this will not "work" when man has advanced spiritually and knows a higher law. One cannot turn back, and must put away "graven images."

For example: Two men in my class had had great success in business for several months, when suddenly everything "went to smash." We tried to analyze the situation, and I found, instead of making their affirmations and looking to God for success and prosperity, they had each bought a "lucky monkey." I said: "Oh I see, you have been trusting in the lucky monkeys instead of God." "Put away the lucky monkeys and call on the law of forgiveness," for man has power to forgive or neutralize his mistakes.

They decided to throw the lucky monkeys down a coalhole, and all went well again. This does not mean, however, that one should throw away every "lucky" ornament or horse-shoe about the house, but he must recognize that the power back of it is the one and only power, God, and that the object simply gives him a feeling of expectancy.

I was with a friend, one day, who was in deep despair. In crossing the street, she picked up a horseshoe. Immediately, she was filled with joy and hope. She said God had sent her the horseshoe in order to keep up her courage.

It was indeed, at that moment, about the only thing that could have registered in her consciousness. Her hope became faith, and she ultimately made a wonderful demonstration. I wish to make the point clear that the men previously mentioned were depending on the monkeys, alone, while this woman recognized the power back of the horseshoe.

I know, in my own case, it took a long while to get out of a belief that a certain thing brought disappointment. If the thing happened, disappointment invariably followed. I found the only way I could make a change in the subconscious, was by asserting, "There are not two powers, there is only one power, God, therefore, there are not disappointments, and this thing means a happy surprise." I noticed a change at once, and happy surprises commenced coming my way.

I have a friend who said nothing could induce her to walk under a ladder. I said, "If you are afraid, you are giving in to a belief in two powers, Good and Evil, instead of one. As God is absolute, there can be no opposing power, unless man makes the false of evil for himself. To show you believe in only One Power, God, and that there is no power or reality in evil, walk under the next ladder you see."

Soon after, she went to her bank. She wished to open her box in the safe-deposit vault, and there stood a ladder on her pathway. It was impossible to reach the box without passing under the ladder. She quailed with fear and turned back. She could not face the lion on her pathway. However, when she reached the street, my words rang in her ears and she decided to return and walk under it. It was a big moment in her life, for ladders had held her in bondage for years. She retraced her steps to the vault, and the ladder was no longer there! This so often happens! If one is willing to do a thing he is afraid to do, he does not have to.

It is the law of non-resistance, which is so little understood.

Someone has said that courage contains genius and magic. Face a situation fearlessly, and there is no situation to face; it falls away of its own weight.

The explanation is, that fear attracted the ladder on the woman's pathway, and fearlessness removed it.

Thus the invisible forces are ever working for man who is always "pulling the strings" himself, though he does not know it. Owing to the vibratory power of words, whatever man voices, he begins to attract. People who continually speak of disease, invariably attract it.

After man knows the truth, he cannot be too careful of his words. For example: I have a friend who often says on the 'phone, "Do come to see me and have an old-fashioned chat." This "old-fashioned chat" means an hour of about five hundred to a thousand destructive words, the principal topics being loss, lack, failure and sickness.

I reply: "No, I thank you. I've had enough old-fashioned chats in my life, they are too expensive, but I will be glad to have a new-fashioned chat, and talk about what we want, not what we don't want."

There is an old saying that man only dares use his words for three purposes, to "heal, bless or prosper." What man says of others will be said of him, and what he wishes for another, he is wishing for himself.

"Curses, like chickens, come home to roost."

If a man wishes someone "bad luck," he is sure to attract bad luck himself. If he wishes to aid someone to success, he is wishing and aiding himself to success.

The body may be renewed and transformed through the spoken word and clear vision, and disease be completely wiped out of the consciousness. The metaphysician knows that all disease has a mental correspondence, and in order to heal the body one must first "heal the soul."

The soul is the subconscious mind, and it must be "saved" from wrong thinking.

In the twenty-third psalm, we read: "He restoreth my soul." This means that the subconscious mind or soul, must be restored with the right ideas, and the 'mystical marriage" is the marriage of the soul and the spirit, or the subconscious and superconscious mind. They must be one. When the subconscious is flooded with the perfect ideas of the superconscious, God and man are one, "I and the Father are one." That is, he is one with the realm of perfect ideas; he is the man made in God's likeness and image (imagination) and is given power and dominion over all created things, his mind, body and affairs.

It is safe to say that all sickness and unhappiness come from the violation of the law of love. A new commandment I give unto you, "Love one another," and in the Game of Life, love or good-will takes every trick.

For example: A woman I know, had, for years an appearance of a terrible skin disease. The doctors told her it was incurable, and she was in despair. She was on the stage, and she feared she would soon have to give up her profession, and she had no other means of support. She, however, procured a good engagement, and on the opening night, made a great "hit." She received flattering notices from the critics, and was joyful and elated.

The next day she received a notice of dismissal. A man in the cast had been jealous of her success and had caused her to be sent away. She felt hatred and resentment taking complete possession of her, and she cried out, "Oh God don't let me hate that man." That night she worked for hours "in the silence."

She said, "I soon came into a very deep silence. I seemed to be at peace with myself, with the man, and with the whole world. I continued this for two following nights, and on the third day I found I was healed completely of the skin disease!" In asking for love, or good will, she had fulfilled the law, ("for love is the fulfilling of the law") and the disease (which came from subconscious resentment) was wiped out.

Continual criticism produces rheumatism, as critical, inharmonious thoughts cause unnatural deposits in the blood, which settle in the joints.

False growths are caused by jealousy, hatred unforgiveness, fear, etc. Every disease is caused by a mind not at ease. I said once, in my class, "There is no use asking anyone 'What's the matter with you?' we might just as well say, 'Who's the matter with you?'" "Unforgiveness is the most prolific cause of disease. It will harden arteries or liver, and affect the eye-sight. In its train are endless ills.

I called on a woman, one day, who said she was ill from having eaten a poisoned oyster. I replied, "Oh, no, the oyster was harmless, you poisoned the oyster. What's the matter with you?" She answered, "Oh about nineteen people." She had quarreled with nineteen people and had become so inharmonious that she attracted the wrong oyster.

Any inharmony on the external, indicates there is mental inharmony. "As the within, so the without."

Man's only enemies are within himself. "And a man's foes shall be they of his own household." Personality is one of the last enemies to be overcome, as this planet is taking its initiation in love. It was Christ's message - "Peace on Earth, good will towards man." The enlightened man, therefore, endeavors to perfect himself upon his neighbor. His work is with himself, to send out goodwill and blessings to every man, and the marvelous thing is, that if one blesses a man he has no power to harm him.

For example: A man came to me asking to "treat" for success in business. He was selling machinery, and rival appeared on the scene with what he proclaimed, was a better machine, and my friend feared defeat. I said, "First of all, we must wipe out all fear, and know that God protects your interest, and that the divine idea must come out of the situation. That is, the right machine will be sold, by the right man, to the right man." And I added, "Don't hold one critical thought towards that man. Bless him all day, and be willing not to sell your machine, if it isn't the divine idea." So he went to the meeting, fearless and non-resistant, and blessing the other man. He said the outcome was very remarkable. The other man's machine refused to work, and he sold his without the slightest difficulty. "But I say unto you, love your enemies, bless them that curse you, do good to them that hate you, and pray for them which spitefully use you and persecute you."

"Good-will produces a great aura of protection about the one who sends it, and "No weapon that is formed against him shall prosper." In other words, love and good-will destroy the enemies with one's self, therefore, one has no enemies on the external!" There is peace on earth for him who sends good-will to man!"

Workbook Session Three - The Power of the Word

In this session:

- Energy: Words and Thoughts
- In God Man has Power
- The Law of Non-Resistance
- Fear is an Illusion
- Become a Miracle Magnet
- Man's Enemies – Bless Them
- Negativity and Physical Ailments
- Recap and Journal Pages

Begin this session by asking Archangel Michael to surround you with God's Divine White Light of Protection and set your intention to connect with your higher self – the God Part within.

Father, Mother, God, Creator of All That Is...

I claim my personal power and open the way to see clearly my field of potentiality, my field of infinite possibilities. I cut the ties of beliefs and thought patterns that no longer serve me in all directions of time thereby removing them from my consciousness, my subconscious and my superconscious. I fearlessly step into the magnificence of the true essence of who I am – One with God. I graciously accept all that is mine by divine right, under grace in a miraculous way and commit to fulfill all that I came to be, have and do in this incarnation on Mother Earth at this time.

Amen

Ask your guides, angels and teachers to be present with you to help you open your heart, mind and spirit to the infinite possibilities.

Man has the power to become a magnet for Abundance!

ENERGY: WORDS AND THOUGHTS

We're learning that words and thoughts create our reality – that it is up to us as to whether they create wonderful situations in our lives or disaster. Conscious effort is required to change the conditioned thought processes that we are accustomed to.

The previous chapters/sessions have referenced our deep seated beliefs, thought patterns and fears. Florence addresses the cause and affect of records we hold in our subconscious that affect our daily lives. She points out the affirmations we use that we don't think of as powerful, but they are.

Florence shares with us the example of the man who stated he always missed a car and his daughter who stated that she always caught a car. These are affirmations – one negative and one positive. Their words brought into their reality what they expected to happen. His words were negative, her words were positive and each had written into their subconscious mind the outcome.

How many things do we "unconsciously" create in our reality by thoughtlessly using our words to write a negative action in our subconscious?

WORKBOOK ITEM ONE:

Lets evaluate your thought patterns of unconscious creation. When you are looking for a parking place, do you think, feel or say, "I can never find a parking place" or "I always have a parking place up front." Which is it?

Listed below are a few examples of creating reality. Read each situation and the suggested "spoken word" and then write below it what you always think, feel or say on a regular basis. If your thoughts and words are negative, change them now! Make a conscious effort to use the positive viewpoint of these events and discover a magical way of living!

NOTE: The Universe does NOT recognize "not" so the message you are sending out to the Universe when you say, "I hope the bank isn't busy." Is "I hope the bank IS busy."

Magical Thoughts and Words Form - The Subconscious Records

1. On the way to a place where parking must be found. Suggested Spoken Word/Thought: I always get a parking place close to the door.

2. Getting ready to check out at the grocery store or any place that may have a line: Suggested Spoken Word/Thought: I always get in the quickest checkout line.

3. In anticipation of arriving at an appointed time: Suggested Spoken Word/Thought: I always arrive at the appointed time.

4. In anticipation of arriving at the bank: Suggested Spoken Word/Thought: I always get to the bank at the "right" time. (no line to wait in – if so, only minimal instead of backed out the door)

5. In anticipation of a challenging situation. Suggested Spoken Word/Thought: I always know what to say in difficult situations. (as apposed to sticking my foot in my mouth in awkward situations)

6. In anticipation of ordering food: Suggested Spoken Word/Thought: The food I order from a restaurant is always brought to me correctly and is delicious!

Use the following Journal Page to evaluate and write about what you have discovered about your thought processes. Are they typically negative or positive? Or did you discover that you use conjunctive words with "NOT" e.g. "is not – isn't," "do not – doesn't." Did you learn you are continually ordering exactly what you do NOT want from the Universe?

Evaluate your thought patterns. What other affirmations do you regularly make for yourself – are they positive or negative? Write about your findings.

JOURNAL PAGES:

IN GOD MAN HAS POWER

There is only one power – God. Man has a God Part within, so in turn, man has power over the reality of his life.

Florence states that **"Man has the power to forgive or neutralize his mistakes" - "to have dominion over all created things, his mind, body and affairs."**

These are bold statements.

When we realize a source of negativity or mistake, we have the opportunity to neutralize it through reconditioning our subconscious mind. In recognizing this source of negativity, we understand that the thought pattern or belief no longer works for us. Identifying the negative thought pattern is the first step to relieving the source of its power. Now we can eliminate it from our subconscious records. The place left vacant may now be filled with the positive viewpoint of the situation based in love. The source of negativity is neutralized and on the way to healing – no matter what the situation, condition, or thought pattern.

This process was proven in previous workbook exercises when the unconscious negative thought patterns and beliefs were recognized, neutralized and transmuted to positive thought patterns. Each new thought pattern became a new record in the subconscious to be executed at the next available opportunity.

This experience demonstrates the power we have over our thoughts, and reality. It is up to us to consciously monitor these thoughts to maintain a foundation of love. It is up to us to supervise our random thinking in order to live the limitless life that is our birthright. As we integrate love based thoughts and beliefs into our daily lives, monitoring our thoughts becomes a part of us – as easy as breathing.

THE LAW OF NON-RESISTANCE

Florence states that the Law of Non-resistance is "little understood." When we look at it from a point of control, it is easier to understand. Beginning as babies we're taught to be in control of ourselves. It doesn't take us long to want to be in control of others as well as situations and conditions around us.

We are learning to allow our highest good to come to us through "knowing" within that what we desire is ours – this requires non-resistance. After all, we know what we want and we want it now – yes? To be in harmony with God, to be fully connected and show active faith and trust, we must allow God/the Universe to match to us what we have asked for. Patience, faith and trust take practice.

To place an order for food at a restaurant, then allow it to be delivered to us is non-resistant. To release anxiety/fear surrounding a life event, situation or relationship is non-resistant. When we "worry" about our family members and life situations/events we are in "resistance." When we release our worry, fear and expectations of "how" an event or relationship will heal, we are non-resistant.

It is NOT in our best interest to take it back and play with it – taking it back and playing with it negates our non-resistance and we again become resistant.

WORKBOOK ITEM TWO:

You may find handing an important, possibly volatile situation over to God to handle with complete trust and faith is sometimes challenging. In assessing the intricacies of such a situation, you can clearly see the workings and benefits of non-resistance.

Sit quietly and think about a situation you are experiencing that you feel is "out of your control" and causing you anxiety. Write down the situation or event in the appropriate column. Think about how you can dissipate your fear and move into a non-resistant state. What tools will you use – prayer – meditation – writing - affirmations? Then write about the results.

Executing Non-Resistance Form

Situation/Event	Non-resistance Tools	Results

Use the Journal Page to write about the non-resistance experience from beginning to end. Evaluate if you were able to achieve complete non-resistance or if you held on to physical world conditioning and tried to control the situation. Evaluate the results. If you weren't able to reach the non-resistant state, try again. Each time you try you will step up in your level of understanding and it will become easier. This is a powerful and important tool to reach the ultimate level of trust and faith in God.

JOURNAL PAGE:

FEAR IS AN ILLUSION

If we allow fear into our lives, it will begin to control us – as it did the woman who was afraid to walk under a ladder. When she went to the bank, a ladder was in her path so she walked away, failing to accomplish what she went there to do – fear was in control. Then in remembering Florence's words she went back to walk under the ladder, facing her fears, and discovered the ladder was gone!

Fear of ladders literally held this woman in bondage. We allow this to happen to us in so many other ways. We're fearful of looking for another job when we're unhappy where we are working. We allow fear of being alone or of finances to keep us in unhappy relationships. We let fear control where we go and what we do – how we treat others and how we treat ourselves. Is there honor in being in a situation that makes us fearful or unhappy or depressed? We're afraid and worried about what *might* happen.

In growing up, we learn that fear is normal – it becomes a part of us, like breathing. Fear is a conditioning of the physical world, but it is a choice. Albeit, it is usually an unconscious choice, it is still a choice.

Many times, over and over again we find that the things we fear have no validity, they are but an illusion. Like the woman who feared the ladder, when she faced her fears she realized her mind had deceived her into thinking her fear was a tangible object – it wasn't.

Fear is not real – it is an illusion. When we choose to live in fear – we are in essence telling God we believe more in fear than we believe in Him.

Now we have the power to choose, do we want to be fearful? Or do we want to live free of fear with confidence that we live in an abundant universe and are worthy of living the life we truly desire?

WORKBOOK ITEM THREE:

This exercise is designed to bring to your attention how many frivolous things you worry about. Each one of you knows that your worries and fears are very real to you – the physical world conditioning is very powerful – very convincing to take fear seriously and give it your energy. What you must remember is that fear is an illusion. Life happens to you whether you are worrying or not.

What does worry do to enhance your life?

Nothing.

It is your job, your mission, to give to God any situations, conditions and/or people that ignite fear or worry in your heart. This is part of spiritual growth.

Sit quietly and think about what worry feels like. Look back at your day or week. Was there anything that catches your attention with the "worry" feeling? Evaluate how worry made the situation better or didn't and did it enhance your life? Fill in the appropriate columns with your findings.

Why Worry, It'll Never Happen Form

Situation or Event that Caused Worry	Did worry change the situation or event?	Did it enhance your life to worry?

Use the Journal Page to write about your experience with this exercise. What did you learn about yourself? Do you worry excessively? Did you overlook worries or fears from the previous exercises because the ones you discovered now are "normal" and you didn't recognize them as fear and/or worry? Examine your feelings. Use The Sedona Method® of Release on page 277 or the Healing of Love on page 279 to dissolve your fear/worry and heal the life event, situation or relationship.

JOURNAL PAGE:

BECOME A MIRACLE MAGNET

Man is a "magnet" for what he continually thinks about and has deep seated beliefs of. Whether we like it or believe it – this is true – this is the Law of Attraction. The Universe "matches" to us the vibrational frequency we emit. In understanding this, we now realize we have a choice. We can choose to live from a fear base of negativity, doubt and fear attracting more of the same to us or we may choose to live from a love base, maintaining an Attitude of Gratitude attracting more of the same to us.

Living from a basis of love with an Attitude of Gratitude will transform us to a Miracle Magnet!

WORKBOOK ITEM FOUR

Gratitude is a powerful emotion as previously discussed. This exercise is designed to help you bring forth powerful love based emotions at any given time – to help you reach a state of opulence. You can achieve this with the feeling of gratitude. If negative thoughts try to slip in and undermine your focus on what you truly desire, you can use the feelings of gratitude to dissipate them. This works because gratitude is a love based thought and there is no place for fear and/or negativity in love based thoughts.

This exercise is very powerful, yet it is very easy. You can do this at any given time of the day and change what you are a magnet for – negativity or miracles!

Gratitude Exercise

Sit quietly and breathe deeply. Think about things in your life that you are grateful for. Write down at least five of them.

1.

2.

3.

4.

5.

As you think about them, one by one, allow yourself to experience the feelings of gratitude. Allow the feeling to grow in your body. Identify what they feel like. Allow yourself to feel the gratitude from your core till the feeling encompasses your entire being.

Continue to breathe deeply and be grateful. Thank God/The Universe for all that you are grateful for.

Incorporate this exercise into your daily routine. A few minutes daily of profound gratitude will change your life!

Consciously include these feelings of gratitude to your archive of love based feelings. With practice visioning what you desire and being grateful for the vision, you will be able to reach a place of being grateful for having received *before* you receive. It is at this time that your vibration will be at its highest. You will be a VERY strong magnet for what you desire. Be sure to monitor your Sponsoring Thoughts carefully so that you magnetize to you your desires and not some wayward thoughts of lack and fear. Your sponsoring thought being the root of your thoughts – fear or love.

You have thousands of thoughts every day. The challenge to keep track of every single one of them would leave you no time to do anything else. Setting the intention to live a love based life and implementing all these tools shifts you from living your life unconsciously to living your life consciously.

MAN'S ENEMIES – BLESS THEM

Florence states, "Man's only enemies are within himself." For many of us it is easy to be resentful of someone who has something nicer than we do. But resentment strips us of our power and we hand it with a flourish – to the one we resent. This is true of not only resentment, but also of anger, jealousy, and holding harsh feelings toward someone for offending us. This just doesn't sound right because "they" are the ones, who did something to us, but in reality, they've moved on with their lives – we're the ones suffering from past issues. Resentment can send us on a downward spiral leading to jealousy and self loathing – negative, negative, negative!

As a result we then become a magnet for still more negativity! Without question, our subconscious and the Universal Supply Warehouse will "match" to us more negativity.

We made the "unconscious" choice – yes, it is a choice – to give our power to someone else and allow ourselves to be crippled and vulnerable to outside influences.

Florence reminds us of Matthew 5:43-45: "But I say unto you, love your enemies, bless them that curse you, do good to them that hate you, and pray for them which spitefully use you and persecute you."

The operative word here is "bless." Florence suggests to us to "Bless him all day." She teaches us that "if one blesses a man he has no power to harm him." This is a true, valid statement.

This workbook goes a step farther. We suggest *"Blessing him **sincerely from the heart** all day!"*

WORKBOOK ITEM FIVE

Breathe deeply, sit quietly and think about the act of giving your power away to people after a confrontation, situation or event.

Note: You will know you've given your power away when you think of a situation and it still upsets you to think about it.

Step outside the situation and evaluate the catalyst that prompted you to give away your power. Then look deeply within and find the feeling you experienced when you released your power – you were lost immediately to miserable feelings – yes? And what was worse you experience those feelings again every time you think about the person, situation or event.

Write down in the Event/Catalyst to Giving Away Your Power column what the event was. Then ask your guides and angels to help you to *bless sincerely* the person you gave your power to. Write what you experience in the Blessing Experience column. When you first do this you may not feel anything – do it again. Continue to bless this person *sincerely from the heart* repeatedly until you feel the anxiousness within you dissipate. You will feel lighter, happier, and more joyful – you will even begin to feel *love* for this person. Not a romantic love – a love of God. This will take patience and repetition.

Blessing Form

Event/Catalyst to giving away your power	Blessing Experience

By setting the intent to bless the negative we set in motion the change of our perspective. In following through by blessing the negativity *sincerely from the heart* we disintegrate its power and transmute the situation from one of fear to one of *love*. In the process we become non-resistant.

You may also use the Healing Circle of Love to heal this life situation, event or relationship. Use the Journal Page to write about your experience with this exercise.

This is an intensely powerful tool. It isn't an easy tool to use, because if we're upset with someone, the last thing we really want to do is bless them. That's why *sincerely blessing them* is so important. We must be sincere or it's just lip service. Put the "sincerely from the heart" energy behind it!

Know that living in the abundance you desire is a choice and using this tool will help you get there – don't let the level of your emotions toward another person get between you and God. Everything is a choice – make the best one for you.

JOURNAL PAGE

NEGATIVITY AND PHYSICAL AILMENTS

Florence tells us that "the body may be renewed and transformed through the spoken word and clear vision, and disease be completely wiped out of the consciousness. The metaphysician knows that all disease has a mental correspondence, and in order to heal the body one must first *heal the soul. All sickness and unhappiness come from the violation of the law of love.*" She further states that, "continual criticism produces rheumatism, as critical, inharmonious thoughts cause unnatural deposits in the blood, which settle in the joints. False growths are caused by jealously, hatred, unforgiveness, fear, etc. Every disease is caused by a mind not at ease" and "unforgiveness is the most prolific cause of disease." "Any inharmony on the external indicates there is mental inharmony."

These are bold statements.

The Law of Love tells us "Love one another." We all know what it feels like to be angry with someone, to feel jealousy and resentment. These feelings are not fun. They rob us of our joy and strip away our happiness. If these emotions are practiced on a daily basis, we forget to honor others and we certainly don't honor ourselves. The negativity of the emotion begins to gnaw at us and hold us captive. Our minds lose clarity and our physical body begins to suffer the consequences.

By understanding more of the ceaseless interaction of cause and effect, it begins to make sense that inharmony within can cause illness within the physical body.

Worry, anxiety, anger, jealousy, resentment and hatred are mental self poisoning emotions and thought patterns. Choosing to indulge in these feelings and thoughts maintains a state of chronic self-poisoning that destroys happiness, blocks the connection with God, leaves the body susceptible to illness and disease and can untimely shorten the life of the physical body.

The physical world "teaches" us that living in a constant, continual state of inharmony and discord is "normal." This is a form of Physical World Conditioning. Know that this is a choice – that each one of us *has* the choice and *makes* the choice to live in discord and inharmony in a fear base. It is up to us to choose to transmute - to change - the negative patterns and emotions to love base thoughts and beliefs.

The Game of Life and this workbook are full of tools to aid in dissipating toxic thought patterns, beliefs and habits.

Now that our eyes are opened to the reality of negative fear based thoughts drawing to us a life that is less than we truly desire, we are better able to make good choices for our highest good.

We are now able to see clearly how fear based living will take its toll on the body. "Heal Your Life" by Louise Hay is another excellent tool to help identify fear based issues within the body.

Make the conscious choices to use daily the tools provided here. Be open to receive the additional tools to rid yourself of suppressed fear based thoughts and beliefs so that you may live a healthy, happy, joy filled life of miracles!

It is your choice!

RECAP

The information contained in Power of The Word sheds light on the day to day "unconscious" records we have instilled in our subconscious. Florence has given us tools to recognize and transmute the negativity to positivity.

In traveling through your day, keep in mind the intention to integrate the three levels of consciousness. When an event or situation based in fear comes your way, use the tools you've leaned here to dissipate it – work in conjunction with God to allow Him to handle it. This will leave you free to continue your day in harmony. Life will be calmer, more joyful and when you've truly mastered faith and trust in God, stress free. Can you imagine your life stress free?

It is your choice.

Honor yourself and God in all that you do – allow yourself to be One with God – it is a choice. Monitor your thoughts, words and actions – are they love based or fear based? Remember, they are one or the other – never both!

Journal daily if possible the changes you are experiencing within you. Also take note and journal the changes – the blessings – that are filling your life. God is truly lighting your Divine Life path – allow His love to guide you in all that you do. Graciously accept and acknowledge the blessings that bathe your life and pay the gifts forward to others…

Be sure to thank your guides, teachers and angels for being in attendance and helping you to clearly understand God's guidance.

May you be profoundly blessed in this moment and in every moment after…

JOURNAL PAGE:

"Resist not evil. Be not overcome of evil, but overcome evil with good."

Nothing on earth can resist an absolutely non-resistant person.

The Chinese say that water is the most powerful element, because it is perfectly non-resistant. It can wear away a rock, and sweep all before it.

Jesus Christ said, "Resist not evil," for He knew in reality, there is no evil, therefore nothing to resist. Evil has come of man's "vain imagination," or a belief in two powers, good and evil.

There is an old legend, that Adam and Eve ate of "Maya the Tree of Illusion," and saw two powers instead of one power, God.

Therefore, evil is a false law man has made for himself, through psychoma or soul sleep. Soul sleep means, that man's soul has been hypnotized by the race belief (of sin, sickness and death, etc.) which is carnal or mortal thought, and his affairs have out-pictured his illusions.

We have read in a preceding chapter, that man's soul is his subconscious mind, and whatever he feels deeply, good or bad, is outpictured by that faithful servant. His body and affairs show forth what he has been picturing. The sick man has pictured sickness, the poor man, poverty, the rich man, wealth.

People often say, "why does a little child attract illness, when it is too young even to know what it means?"

I answer that children are sensitive and receptive to the thoughts of others about them, and often outpicture the fears of their parents.

I heard a metaphysician once say, "If you do not run your subconscious mind yourself, someone else will run it for you."

Mothers often, unconsciously, attract illness and disaster to their children, by continually holding them in thoughts of fear, and watching for symptoms.

For example: A friend asked a woman if her little girl had had the measles. She replied promptly, "not yet!" This implied that she was expecting the illness, and therefore, preparing the way for what she did not want for herself and child.

However, the man who is centered and established in right thinking, the man who sends out only good-will to his fellow-man, and who is without fear, cannot be *touched or influenced by the negative thoughts of others.* In fact, he could then receive only good thoughts, as he himself, sends forth only thoughts.

Resistance is Hell, for it places man in a "state of torment."

A metaphysician once gave me a wonderful recipe for taking every trick in the game of life, it is the acme of non-resistance. He gave it in this way: "At one time in my life, I baptized children, and of course, they had many names. Now I no longer baptize children, but I baptize events, but *I give every event the same name.* If I have a failure I baptize it success, in the name of the Father, and of the Son, and of the Holy Ghost!"

In this, we see the great law of transmutation, founded on non-resistance. Through his spoken word, every failure was transmuted into success.

For example: A woman who required money, and who knew the spiritual law of opulence, was thrown continually in a business-way, with a man who made her feel very poor. He talked lack and limitation and she commenced to catch his poverty thoughts, so she disliked him, and blamed him for her failure. She knew in order to demonstrate her supply, she must first feel that she *had received - a feeling of opulence must precede its manifestation.*

It dawned on her, one day, that she was resisting the situation, and seeing two powers instead of one. So she blessed the man and baptized the situation "Success"! She affirmed, "As there is only one power, God, this man is here for my good and my prosperity" (just what he did not seem to be there for). Soon after that she met, *through this man,* a woman who gave her for a service rendered, several thousand dollars, and the man moved to a distant city, and faded harmoniously from her life. Make the statement, "Every man is a golden link in the chain of my good," for all men are God in manifestation, *awaiting the opportunity given by man, himself, to serve the divine plan of his life.*

"Bless your enemy, and you rob him of his ammunition." His arrows will be transmuted into blessings.

This law is true of nations as well as individuals. Bless a nation, send love and good-will to every inhabitant, and it is robbed of its power to harm.

Man can only get the right idea of non-resistance, through spiritual understanding. My students have often said: "I don't want to be a door-mat." I reply "when you use non-resistance with wisdom, no one will ever be able to walk over you."

Another example: One day I was impatiently awaiting an important telephone call. I resisted every call that came in and made no out-going calls myself, reasoning that it might interfere with the one I was awaiting.

Instead of saying, "Divine ideas never conflict, the call will come at the right time," leaving it to Infinite Intelligence to arrange, I commenced to manage things myself - I made the battle mine, not God's and remained tense and anxious. The bell did not ring for about an hour, and I glanced at the 'phone and found the receiver had been off that length of time, and the 'phone was disconnected. My anxiety, fear and belief in interference, had brought on a total eclipse of the telephone. Realizing what I had done, I commenced blessing the situation at once; I baptized it "success," and affirmed, "I cannot lose any call that belongs to me by divine right; I am under *grace, and not under law.*"

A friend rushed out to the nearest telephone, to notify the Company to reconnect.

She entered a crowded grocery, but the proprietor left his customers and attended to the call himself. My 'phone was connected at once, and two minutes later, I received a very important call, and about an hour afterward, the one I had been awaiting.

One's ships come in over a calm sea.

So long as man resists a situation, he will have it with him. If he runs away from it, it will run after him.

For example: I repeated this to a woman one day, and she replied, "How true that is! I was unhappy at home, I disliked my mother, who was critical and domineering; so I ran away and was married - but I married my mother, for my husband was exactly like my mother, and I had the same situation to face again." "Agree with thine adversary quickly."

This means, agree that the adverse situation is good, be undisturbed by it, and it falls away of its own weight. "None of these things move me," is a wonderful affirmation.

The inharmonious situation comes from some inharmony within man himself.

When there is, in him, no emotional response to an inharmonious situation, it fades away forever, from his pathway.

So we see man's work is ever with himself.

People have said to me, "Give treatments to change my husband, or my brother." I reply, "No, I will give *treatments to change you;* when you change, your husband and your brother will change."

One of my students was in the habit of lying. I told her it was a failure method and if she lied, she would be lied to. She replied, "I don't care, I can't possibly get along without lying."

One day she was speaking on the 'phone to a man with whom she was very much in love. She turned to me and said, "I don't trust him, I know he's lying to me." I replied, "Well, you lie yourself, so someone has to lie to you, and you will be sure it will be just the person you want the truth from." Some time after that, I saw her, and she said, "I'm cured of lying."

I questioned: "What cured you?"

She replied: "I have been living with a woman who lied worse than I did!"

One is often cured of his faults by seeing them in others.

Life is a mirror, and we find only ourselves reflected in our associates.

Living in the past is a failure method and a violation of spiritual law.

Jesus Christ said, "Behold, now is the accepted time." "Now is the day of Salvation."

Lot's wife looked back and was turned into a pillar of salt.

The robbers of time are the past and the future. Man should bless the past, and forget it, if it keeps him in bondage, and bless the future, knowing it has in store for him endless joys, but live *fully in the now.*

For example: A woman came to me, complaining that she had no money with which to buy Christmas gifts. She said, "Last year was so different; I had plenty of money and gave lovely presents, and this year I have scarcely a cent."

I replied, "You will never demonstrate money while you are pathetic and live in the past. Live fully in the *now,* and *get ready to give Christmas presents.* Dig your ditches, and the money will come." She exclaimed, "I know what to do! I will buy some tinsel twine, Christmas seals and wrapping paper." I replied, "Do that, and the *presents will come and stick themselves to the Christmas seals."*

This too, was showing financial fearlessness and faith in God, as the reasoning mind said, "Keep every cent you have, as you are not sure you will get any more."

She bought the seals, paper and twine, and a few days before Christmas, received a gift of several hundred dollars. Buying the seals and twine had impressed the subconscious with expectancy, and opened the way for the manifestation of the money. She purchased all the presents in plenty of time.

Man must live suspended in the moment.

"Look well, therefore, to this Day! Such is the salutation of the Dawn."

He must be spiritually alert, ever awaiting his leads, taking advantage of every opportunity.

One day, I said continually (silently), "Infinite Spirit, don't let me miss a trick," and something very important was told to me that evening. It is most necessary to begin the day with right words.

Make an affirmation immediately upon waking.

For example: *"Thy will be done this day! Today is a day of completion, I give thanks for this perfect day, miracle shall follow miracle and wonders shall never cease."*

Make this a habit, and one will see wonders and miracles come into his life.

One morning I picked up a book and read, "Look with wonder at that which is before you!" It seemed to be my message for the day, so I repeated again and again, "Look with wonder at that which is before you."

At about noon, a large sum of money, was given me, which I had been desiring for a certain purpose.

In a following chapter, I will give affirmations that I have found most effective. However, one should never use an affirmation unless it is absolutely satisfying and convincing to his own consciousness, and often an affirmation is changed to suit different people.

For example: The following has brought success to many: "I have a wonderful work, in a wonderful way, I give wonderful service, for wonderful pay!"

I gave the first two lines to one of my students, and she added the last two.

It made a *most powerful statement,* as there should always be perfect payment for perfect service, and a rhyme sinks easily into the subconscious. She went about singing it aloud and soon did receive wonderful work in a wonderful way, and gave wonderful service for wonderful pay.

Another student, a business man, took it, and changed the word work to business. He repeated, "I have a wonderful business, in a wonderful way, and I give wonderful service for wonderful pay." That afternoon he made a forty-one thousand dollar deal, though there had been no activity in his affairs for months.

Every affirmation must be carefully worded and completely "cover the ground."

For example: I knew a woman, who was in great need, and made a demand for work. She received a great deal of work, but was never paid anything. She now knows to add, "Wonderful service for wonderful pay."

It is man's divine right to have plenty! More than enough!

"His barns should be full, and his cup should flow over!" This is God's idea for man, and when man breaks down the barriers of lack in his own consciousness, the Golden Age will be his, and every righteous desire of his heart fulfilled!

Workbook Session Four - The Law of Non-Resistance

In this session:

- What is Evil?
- The Law of Attraction
- The Law of Transmutation
- Dissipating Inharmony
- Living in the Moment
- Affirmations/Expectancy
- I Allow Myself to Receive
- Recap and Journal Pages

Begin this session by asking Archangel Michael to surround you with God's Divine White Light of Protection and set your intention to connect with your higher self – the God Part within.

Father, Mother, God, Creator of All That Is…

I claim my personal power and open the way to see clearly my field of potentiality, my field of infinite possibilities. I cut the ties of beliefs and thought patterns that no longer serve me in all directions of time thereby removing them from my consciousness, my subconscious and my superconscious. I fearlessly step into the magnificence of the true essence of who I am – One with God. I graciously accept all that is mine by divine right, under grace in a miraculous way and commit to fulfill all that I came to be, have and do in this incarnation on Mother Earth at this time.

Amen

Ask your guides, angels and teachers to be present with you to help you open your heart, mind and spirit to the infinite possibilities.

Jesus Christ said, "Resist not Evil," for He knew in reality,
there is no evil, therefore there is nothing to resist.

WHAT IS EVIL?

When we experience complete faith and trust in God throughout our three levels of consciousness, we know that there is no evil. We will have experienced from within the true one power – God and we will understand we are One with Him.

Man teaches each other that there are two powers – God and Evil. Florence teaches us that "carnal or mortal thought" – physical world conditioning – takes over our subconscious and superconscious convincing us that fear is normal thereby, excommunicating us from our God source.

If we must put a face to Evil, it is physical world conditioning.

We know from our own lives that we have taken these teachings and allowed them to "outpicture" the God Part within us. We prove this by effectively manifesting lack to the point of poverty as well as other forms of fearful situations. If there is a part of our square of life that is less than what we desire, it is because we have allowed the physical world conditionings of earth to have control of our lives – our subconscious, thereby controlling our superconscious – the God Part.

Another truth that Florence points out is that if we aren't in control of our consciousness, then others will be. We are all sensitive beings who can be influenced by the energies of others. If we are in concert with the three levels of consciousness – One with God, we cannot be influenced by the physical world of fear.

It is our job, our mission, to be in control of our thoughts and beliefs in conjunction with God. It is also our mission to base our thoughts and beliefs in love.

As sensitive spiritual beings it is up to us to hold fast to the one power - God. It is this belief in one power that protects us from fear and worry. It is this belief that protects us from negativity. "The man who is centered and established in right thinking, the man who sends out only good-will to his fellow man, and who is without fear, cannot be touched or influenced by the negative thoughts of others."

It is easy to take in the negativity of others. If we allow ourselves to believe in fear or evil as a power like God, it will be impossible to integrate our three levels of consciousness and we will be doomed to a life feeling scattered and lost in chaos.

THE LAW OF ATTRACTION

We have learned that our thoughts, words and actions are what create the reality of our lives. What we continually think about we become a magnet for. As we grow and develop on our spiritual journey, we will find that we become magnets for like minded people. They will find us in amazing ways. Just as when we work in tandem with the three levels of consciousness – abundance that we desire will also find us in amazing ways.

Use the Law of Attraction wisely – monitor your thoughts so that they are based in love and gratitude – not fear – for if they are fear based, that is what you will be a magnet for – negativity and fear. Work with the God Part within to discern what is in your highest good and allow God, in His infinite wisdom to deliver to you that highest good.

Most people do not understand the Law of Attraction and use it to bring chaos, confusion, disharmony and negativity into their lives. We are constantly in a ceaseless interaction of cause and effect. Through our thoughts, words and beliefs we create the energy within us of love or of fear and we attract more of it to us.

In learning the Laws of the Universe, we are elevated to a higher level of understanding. Utilize this information to the fullest possible extent. Work closely with God and experience the magical changes love brings.

WORKBOOK ITEM ONE

This exercise is designed to bring to light the thoughts that sneak in and sabotage us. Sit quietly, and honestly look at your thought processes. Is there something in your life that seems to be repeating that is negative? Example: Do you get a cold every winter? In the recesses of your mind do you think, "I get a cold every winter"?

This is the Law of Attraction. We attract a cold through our thoughts/beliefs. The thoughts/beliefs put us at a lower, fear based frequency and the universe "matches" to us that frequency – "lower fear base frequency of a cold."

It isn't enough to just change the words – the words must be believed from deep within.

In the world of Divine Mind, there is no reason for a person to get a cold every winter. Some people work in the cold and get wet, but never get a cold. There is no disease or illness in Divine Mind. Therefore, if we are connected to our God Part within and working in tandem with the three levels of consciousness, germs of a cold cannot stick to us. Our vibrational frequency will be higher than that of the vibrational frequency of the germ; thereby, we will repel one another.

Evaluate your thought processes. Identify a negative thought pattern or belief that you have. Look closely – you'll find one – perhaps it is gossip. When you gossip about others, others gossip about you. Write it down in the Negative Thought column. Then write about the negativity that has been attracted to you through this form of negativity. Transmute it to positive. It may be necessary to invoke The Sedona Method® of Release and/or the Healing Circle of Love to transmute the negative thought, word or action – use the tools necessary.

After you've experienced how the Law of Attraction works with negative thoughts, then experience it with positive thought. A positive example is: "I'm always healthy."

Think about your life and assess your thought patterns to discern which ones are positive. Identify the things that are attracted to you through the positive energy evoked from the thought pattern.

Thought Monitoring Form

Negative Thought	Identify what you Attracted
Positive Thought	Identify what you Attracted

Do you now see clearly the power of your thought processes?

Use the Journal Page to write about your experience of the Law of Attraction. As you journal, you will see more clearly how The Law of Attraction has been working in your life from an unconscious level. Evaluate honestly your thought patterns and implement the changes necessary to make them love based, thereby attracting to you all that is good.

Using the Law of Attraction wisely is a choice. Now that you have learned that your thoughts, beliefs and actions create your reality, you are consciously choosing whether your life is positive, love based and filled with the abundance you desire or negative, fear based and filled with the abundance you do not desire.

JOURNAL PAGE:

WORKBOOK ITEM TWO

Now that you have identified yet more sneaky negative, fear based thought patterns, use The Sedona Method® of Release on page 277 and/or the Healing Circle of Love on page 279 to dissipate and heal the thought patterns from the previous exercise.

Use the Journal Page to write about your experience in releasing the negativity from your square of life.

JOURNAL PAGE:

THE LAW OF TRANSMUTATION

Florence explains The Law of Transmutation using the example of the man who claimed everything he did as "Success" even if in the judgment of the physical world it wasn't. In his mind he saw everything as success, therefore, it was.

In claiming everything as "Success" the man also invoked the Law of Attraction in a love based, positive way, attracting to him "Success!"

She also uses the example of the woman who found herself catching a man's feelings of lack and poverty. As a result she disliked him. She discovered she was "resisting" the situation. She transmuted the situation by claiming him "a golden link in her chain of good, for all men are God in manifestation."

In the previous session, Power of The Word, we experienced the Blessing Form, Workbook Item Four. This too is an example of transmutation. In "blessing our perceived enemies it transmutes the arrows used to hurt us into blessings."

Florence explains that the only way to understand fully the Law of Transmutation is through spiritual understanding/enlightenment. There is a positive aspect or perfection in every situation – no matter what the situation. Getting our mind around this isn't easy. We tend to believe that some things have nothing good about them – like death. We are taught to believe that death is bad. In reality our spirit is joining God and other deceased loved ones. We are reunited with a love so profound the human mind cannot take it in – how can this be bad?

In assessing frustrating things that happen to us, we must realize that all is in divine order – everything. If we're stuck in traffic, that is where we are supposed to be. We've heard that on 911 there was a man who wore new shoes to work and got a blister before he got there. He stopped to purchase a Band-Aid and put it on his foot. This made him late enough to his office that he was not in the World Trade Center when it collapsed. He was in the right place at the right time.

In accepting that all is in divine order and that we are all in the "right" place at the "right" time, we will eliminate a tremendous amount of stress from our lives. Transmute the anxiety to peacefulness by accepting All is in Divine Order.

NOTE: Keep in mind, as discussed previously, *blessing* seeming adversity transmutes a situation from fear to love thereby, attracting to us the love based vibration of the blessing – not the negative fear based vibration of the adversity!

WORKBOOK ITEM THREE

Previously we identified negative life situations or relationships and used the Healing Circle of Love or The Sedona Method® of Release to transmute your fear to love. You did your best to transmute all the negative situations and relationships to a source of love thereby healing them.

However, as a spiritual being experiencing a human existence you have two things that go on continually: 1) you live in a physical world where daily life is laced with negative assaults to your spiritual being-ness. 2) you are now open to evolving and ascending to a higher level of consciousness, thereby revealing more and more layers of fear that must be addressed.

This exercise is designed to help us transmute situations from negative to positive. Breathe deeply, sit quietly and think about a negative situation, person or event.

Use the Transmutation Form to identify the negative fear based life events, situations or relationships and use the Healing Circle of Love tool to transmute it to a positive, healed situation, event or relationship based in love.

Transmutation Form

Negative Situation, Event or Relationship to Transmute to Love

Use the Journal Page to write about your experience with transmutation using the Healing Circle of Love. With the aid of your guides and angels you will find the good in the situation. In transmuting the experience to positive from negative, you will find great peace and comfort. You will be free to move forward with your life unburdened previous negativity.

Again, this tool is very, very powerful. Use it often – make it a part of your every day life to let go of the stressful moments. You will find living from a foundation of love much, much easier!

JOURNAL PAGE:

DISSIPATING INHARMONY

Florence teaches us that in resisting a situation it will stay with us. If we run away from a situation, it will follow us. When faced with an event that our first impulse is to resist – such as an inharmonious situation, we must transmute our feelings to those of harmony. We want to change our feelings of adversity to feelings free of anxiety – we want to reach a state of being undisturbed.

In facing situations of inharmony, we must look deeper to discover why we are experiencing the anxious inharmonious feelings within. Florence teaches that the inharmony is based "within man himself." It is our perception – our thoughts - of a situation that create the inharmony within us.

We have chosen to allow ourselves to have disagreeable feelings about a situation or person. To dissipate the inharmony, we must achieve a state of no emotional response to the situation. To do this we must live from a source of love – our three levels of consciousness working in tandem as a team. It is then that we will stop resisting situations and fully give them to God to heal.

We must remember, we do not have the control to change a situation, however; we have complete power over how we react, feel and think about a situation. When we connect with the disharmony within us and stop resisting the situation, the situation will change.

How do we move from feelings of inharmony to a source of love with no emotional response?

The first step is to take a deep breath and acknowledge we are feeling the inharmony – not just keep on with our day as if nothing happened. When ignore a situation, we stuff the inharmony and implode later – not a good idea. *Identify and Acknowledge inharmony!*

Transmuting inharmony is twofold. Florence states that "life is a mirror, and we find only ourselves reflected in our associates." This statement is not easy to take in. We don't like to think that the characteristics and behaviors we don't like in others are the characteristics and behaviors that we don't like in ourselves. This just seems wrong. But it is true. Getting our mind around it isn't easy, but when we do and we reach a state of being unemotional, then we can see clearly how to eradicate the characteristic or behavior in ourselves. It is then that we become balanced, more peaceful, more joyful and more confident.

Feeling inharmonious toward others due to something we identify with appears to be a form of control that is misdirected. We want *THEM* to change, when what must happen is to change ourselves.

The following exercise is a tool to help us with situations and other people. It is also a valuable tool to help us eradicate the characteristics and behaviors that we exhibit ourselves that we do not like. We will be able to achieve an unemotional state in which to view ourselves clearly, honestly and from a foundation of love instead of criticism and negativity. This is most important – we are not to judge ourselves, but to elevate ourselves to a higher spiritual level, thereby filling our lives with love and initiating the healing process.

WORKBOOK ITEM FOUR

In the previous exercise you addressed negative situations, events or relationships that are at the forefront of your thoughts. Now you want to address the life situations/events and/or people (inharmonious situations) you have suppressed and/or ignored. Often as a human you cannot "see the forest for the trees" so in order to pull back all layers of fear that make up the human you are in this moment, approach the layers from a different perspective – inharmony.

By looking within inharmonious situations, you will discover what was overlooked before. At first you may think you've transmuted everything – look deeper – perhaps to childhood. You will find something. Snag it, bring it forth and transmute it to love!

Look back at your day or week. Did anything happen that gave you that "angst" feeling in your chest? That tweak of "this isn't right" or "I don't like this" feeling? Identify one situation and write it in the Inharmonious Situation column. Now we will transmute the negativity of the situation to love based feelings that leave us undisturbed.

We may transmute the situation to achieve a non emotional state by using one or both of these tools: Healing Circle of Love or The Sedona Method® of Release.

In the Transmutation Experience column, write about the technique you used and what happened.

Dissipating Inharmony Form

Inharmonious Situation

Use the Journal Page to write about your experiences in completing this exercise. As you journal your thoughts and experiences, you anchor in your subconscious these tools to help you transmute the next inharmonious situation that comes into your life instead of suppressing or ignoring it. The more you do this, the more balanced and stress-free your life will become. You enhance your personal power and build a stronger bridge linking the three levels of consciousness – your bond with God.

JOURNAL PAGE:

LIVING IN THE MOMENT

"Living in the past is a failure method and a violation of spiritual law. Jesus Christ said, "Behold, now is the accepted time. Now is the day of Salvation."

Florence explains to us that "the robbers of time are the past and the future. Man should bless the past, and forget it, for it keeps him in bondage, and bless the future, knowing it has in store for him endless joys, but live fully in the now."

Humans are notorious for dwelling, stewing, and worrying about the past *and* the future. Living in the past and worrying about the future is what we DO. Living in the moment is something we miss. Then the moment is gone.

WORKBOOK ITEM FIVE

This exercise will open our eyes to the time we spend daily fretting about the past or the future and how much *real* time we spend living in this moment. Look back honestly at your day today. Was there a time you were fretting about something that happened in the past – something you did or something perhaps your child, spouse or coworker did? If so, jot it down in the Past column.

Look back honestly at your day and determine if you were fretting or worrying about a future event. Be honest, this could be a future event concerning yourself or the world in general (news programs inspire these kinds of worries quite often). Write about it in the Future column.

Now evaluate your thoughts from the day to determine if there was any time spent experiencing the Now of This Moment. Did you savor the smell of a flower? Did you hold your child close and think of only how good they felt? Did you notice how blue the sky was and be grateful for it? Did you breathe deeply and experience the glory of how good it felt to fill your lungs with air? If you remember doing anything that made you consciously remember the moment, write about it in the NOW column.

Oblivious, is the frightening column… Do you remember the drive home? Do you remember showering? Do you remember feeling alive today? How many moments during the day were you going through the motions oblivious to what you were doing and what was really going on around you. If you experienced this, be honest and write it down in the Oblivious column.

Living In The Moment Form

Past	Future	NOW	Oblivious

This exercise is profoundly eye opening. Use the Journal Page to write about your discoveries and evaluate what changes you can make within you and in your life program to live in the moment of each day. Did you find that when you were experiencing an Attitude of Gratitude that you were living "in the moment?" There is only "this moment" when experiencing gratitude.

In honestly reviewing your daily life, it will become clear how to implement these changes. The key is to make living in the moment your routine – like breathing - to achieve living in the moment as normal behavior instead of occasional behavior.

JOURNAL PAGE:

AFFIRMATIONS/EXPECTANCY

Florence states that "it is most necessary to begin the day with right words." She is reminding us that we bring into our lives what we think of. If we begin the day with negative thoughts, then that is what we are a magnet for – we will manifest negativity, chaos and possibly disaster.

A clear example: I stayed with some friends before moving to Colorado. It was my job to waken the children for elementary school. Each morning I would go to their room and rouse them from sleep telling them what a wonderful day they were going to have. The son was always quite grumpy and one day belligerent as well. Becoming frustrated, I told him, without thinking, that his day would be miserable and left the room. Granted, this was really a terrible thing to do, but the results were amazing. That evening when I got home from work, both of them came to me begging me to never tell them they would have a miserable day – for indeed, it had been. The son was *very* sorry for his grumpiness and would never behave like that again – and he didn't.

This example teaches us:

1. The children were not in control of the three levels of their consciousness, so they were easily influenced. Their subconscious record was written for the day by my words – we DO influence others, especially children – we must be careful that our influence is based in love, not negativity.

2. Our words are powerful – the statement "your day will be miserable" affirmed the day they would have – and they did.

Clearly affirmations can be very powerful. They create expectancy of what is to come and anchors our faith in the receipt. The key to using affirmations is that they must "click" in your truth center to bring forward the most power. As we read an affirmation, we know whether or not it resonates within us. When you feel that warm fuzzy glow within when reading an affirmation – USE IT! You are feeling the acknowledgement of the subconscious that it believes the affirmation – it is written in your record. As we have learned, if it is written in our subconscious record, the subconscious/universe will work to bring it to fruition in our reality.

In using an affirmation that "clicks" we bring together the three levels of consciousness:

* The conscious mind is thinking of and speaking the affirmation.

* The subconscious mind has it recorded and is diligently, tirelessly, working to manifest – we've become a magnet for the affirmation

* The feeling of elation within as we say the affirmation is confirmation of our connection to our God Part – our higher self – working together to receive our highest good. Trust is in place – Faith is in place – we are in receipt - we are One with God.

Florence offers the affirmation for work:

"I have wonderful work, in a wonderful way. I give wonderful service, for wonderful pay!"

Florence points out carefully wording the affirmation to "cover the ground." In the 21st Century we add "with excellent benefits":

"I have wonderful work, in a wonderful way. I give wonderful service, for wonderful pay with excellent benefits!"

This is a specific example of asking "aright."

WORKBOOK ITEM SIX

Affirmations are only words unless they resonate/click deep within you. When this happens they are the catalyst to generating manifestation of what you need or desire. Using affirmations that click with you elevates you to the feeling of opulence – the exhibition of faith and trust that is required to completely integrate the three levels of consciousness to bring into your reality what you desire.

Affirmations are a way to bond with your God Part.

The Affirmation Form below lists a few affirmations. Read through each one and jot down, in the space under the affirmation, the feelings generated by the affirmation. Did the affirmation click? Or did it leave you flat? Rewrite the affirmation to fit your needs.

Then write out a few affirmations of your own that resonate or "click" with you.

AFFIRMATION FORM

God is my supply. Money comes to me easily in unexpected ways by divine right and under grace.

I give thanks for this day, miracle shall follow miracle and wonders shall never cease.

I am an irresistible magnet for all that belongs to me by divine right.

I have wonderful work, in a wonderful way. I give wonderful service, for wonderful pay!
With excellent benefits!

Your Affirmation that resonates or "clicks":

Pick the affirmation that means the most to you to use during the next few days. Repeat it often – put it on a sticky note of the bathroom mirror – the fridge and your computer monitor. Put it in places to remind you.

You've learned how powerful your thoughts and words are. Integrating the daily use of affirmations into your life will help you maintain living from a source of love. Use the Journal Page to write about your experience using the affirmations.

Soul Kisses are spiritual affirmations received daily in your email. If you would like to receive them, please click in to SoulKisses.com.

JOURNAL PAGE:

I ALLOW MYSELF TO RECEIVE

God is a loving God. Florence tells us that "it is man's divine right to have plenty! More than enough! His barns should be full, and his cup should flow over! This is God's idea for man." She has explained to us throughout the chapters that "when man breaks down the barriers of lack in his own consciousness, the Golden Age will be his, and every righteous desire of his heart fulfilled!"

This tells us that artists aren't starving because they are artists, they are starving because they believe they should be starving – the power of their thoughts and words are fulfilled.

We live in an abundant universe. The reality is that we are always living in abundance; however the abundance may be of lack.

Getting our minds around the fact that the abundance we desire is available to us can be challenging due to the teachings of the physical world. It is up to us to cast aside these teachings and look within to discover and discern the God Part within – the superconscious mind – to rewrite the records of our subconscious mind with our findings and monitor the thought patterns, beliefs and words of our conscious mind.

Each one of us has a Field of Potentiality that holds all that we dream of. It is our choice to use tools to dissipate our feelings of unworthiness and living from a source of fear to stepping into our power and living from a source of love.

It is then that we will have eliminated the blocks that prevent us from receiving the abundance we desire. It is a choice to allow ourselves to receive that which we desire or to continue on with limiting thought patterns, beliefs and feelings of unworthiness.

The tools are here – available for use – the choice is ours.

NOTE: It is in our mission to be gracious receivers. *Always* graciously accept gifts from the Universe say Thank You and show gratitude. This promotes universal flow for you and the giver. Refusing receipt will block future universal gifts of abundance for you and the giver!

WORKBOOK ITEM SEVEN

We are each limitless spiritual beings with magnificent Fields of Potentiality. However many of us are beaten down by physical world conditionings and teachings. The Claim Your Power meditation is extremely powerful. It will guide you through the steps of claiming your personal power, embracing it to you and viewing your limitless Field of Potentiality. **Refer to page 287 to experience the Claim Your Power meditation.**

Use the Journal Page to write about your experience and how empowered you are after using it.

JOURNAL PAGE:

RECAP

This chapter, The Law of Non-resistance, is challenging at best. The exercises require us to look at our lives in cold hard honesty – this isn't easy to do. However, if you look closely, you will see the changes you've made in your life from the knowledge in the previous chapters and see that you have, indeed made great progress.

You will also see the healing that has begun. The physical world of earth is not an easy place to live. As we discussed before, as babies we are conditioned to fear, to believe we are limited and to doubt God's love for us. The writings of Florence Scovel Shinn not only help us to walk away from physical world conditioning, but they open the door to healing the pain we have experienced.

The information in this chapter alone, will guide you to a stress-free pathway of living. When the mind gets around transmutation of negativity to a source of love, the doors to endless possibilities are firmly opened. Frivolous worries of the past dissipate leaving us free to enjoy simply breathing while practicing living in the moment opens our eyes to true love and life – *enjoying the experience* of breathing.

You will find that your connection with God has grown tremendously. Look back at your life before you opened this workbook. In your minds eye, travel through your growth. Miraculous isn't it?

Now you have tools to help you maintain balance instead of feeling scattered and flustered. Use these tools. Refresh yourself daily with the tools you've learned. You will find your days less stressful and your life more joyous!

Honor yourself and God in all that you do – allow yourself to fully experience the three levels of consciousness by living in this moment in gratitude. Work closely with God and your entourage of guides, teachers and angels to monitor your thoughts and record only thoughts and beliefs of the highest order in your subconscious. Living from a foundation of love is becoming easier.

Be sure to use the Journal Pages at the end of each session. Be good to yourself and write in them at least ten minutes each day of the things you are discovering, learning and experiencing. As you do this, you will find elation living in your chest – it is the gift of love found in living in the palm of God. You will discover you are moving into a state of receiving avalanches of abundance in all things.

Be sure to thank your guides, teachers and angels for being in attendance and helping you to clearly understand God's work.

May you be profoundly blessed in this moment and in every moment after…

JOURNAL PAGE:

JOURNAL PAGES continued:

Man receives only that which he gives. The Game of Life is a game of boomerangs. Man's thoughts, deeds and words, return to him sooner or later, with astounding accuracy. This is the law of Karma, which is Sanskrit for "Comeback." "Whatsoever a man soweth, that shall he also reap."

For example: A friend told me this story of herself, illustrating the law. She said, "I make all my Karma on my aunt, whatever I say to her, someone says to me. I am often irritable at home, and one day, said to my aunt, who was talking to me during dinner. *'No more talk, I wish to eat in peace.'*"

"The following day, I was lunching with a woman with whom I wished to make a great impression. I was talking animatedly, when she said: *'No more talk, I wish to eat in peace!'*"

My friend is high in consciousness, so her Karma returns much more quickly than to one on the mental plane.

The more man knows, the more he is responsible for, and a person with a knowledge of Spiritual Law, which he does not practice, suffers greatly, in consequence. "The fear of the Lord (law) is the beginning of wisdom." If we read the word Lord, law, it will make many passages in the Bible much clearer. "Vengeance is mine, I will repay saith the Lord" (law). It is the law which takes vengeance, not God. God sees man perfect, "created in his own image," (imagination) and given "power and dominion."

This is the perfect idea of man, registered in Divine Mind, awaiting man's recognition; for man can only be what he sees himself to be, and only attain what he sees himself attaining.

"Nothing ever happens without an on-looker" is an ancient saying.

Man sees first his failure or success, his joy or sorrow, before it swings into visibility from the scenes set in his own imagination. We have observed this in the mother picturing disease for her child, or a woman seeing success for her husband.

Jesus Christ said, "And ye shall know the truth and the truth shall make you free."

So, we see freedom (from all unhappy conditions) comes through knowledge - a knowledge of Spiritual Law.

Obedience precedes authority, and the law obeys man when he obeys the law. The law of electricity must be obeyed before it becomes man's servant. When handled ignorantly, it becomes man's deadly foe. *So with the laws of Mind!*

For example: A woman with a strong personal will, wished she owned a house which belonged to an acquaintance, and she often made mental pictures of herself living in the house. In the course of time, the man died and she moved into the house. Several years afterwards, coming into the knowledge of Spiritual Law, she said to me: "Do you think I had anything to do with that man's death?" I replied: "Yes, your desire was so strong, everything made way for it, but you paid your Karmic debt. Your husband, whom you loved devotedly, died soon after, and the house was a white elephant on your hands for years."

The original owner, however, could not have been affected by her thoughts had he been positive in the truth, nor her husband, but they were both under Karmic law. The woman should have said (feeling the great desire for the house), "Infinite Intelligence, give me the right house, equally as charming as this, the house *which is mine by divine right*."

The divine selection would have given perfect satisfaction and brought good to all. The divine pattern is the only safe pattern to work by.

Desire is a tremendous force, and must be directed in the right channels, or chaos ensues.

In demonstrating, the most important step is the *first step, to "ask aright."*

Man should always demand only that which is his by *divine right.*

To go back to the illustration: Had the woman taken this attitude: "If this house, I desire, is mine, I cannot lose it, if it is not, give me its equivalent," the man might have decided to move out, harmoniously (had it been the divine selection for her) or another house would have been substituted. Anything forced into manifestation through personal will, is always "ill-got," and has "ever bad success."

Man is admonished, "My will be done not thine," and the curious thing is, man always gets just what he desires when he does relinquish personal will, thereby enabling Infinite Intelligence to work through him.

"Stand ye still and see the salvation of the Lord" (law).

For example: A woman came to me in great distress. Her daughter had determined to take a very hazardous trip, and the mother was filled with fear.

She said she had used every argument, had pointed out the dangers to be encountered, and forbidden her to go, but the daughter became more and more rebellious and determined. I said to the mother, "You are forcing your personal will upon your daughter, which you have no right to do, and your fear of the trip is only attracting it, for man attracts what he fears." I added, "Let go, and take your mental hands off; *put it in God's Hands, and use this statement:*" "I put this situation in the hands of

Infinite Love and Wisdom; if this trip is the Divine plan, I bless it and no longer resist, but if it is not divinely planned, I give thanks that it is now dissolved and dissipated."

A day or two after that, her daughter said to her, "Mother, I have given up the trip," and the situation returned to its "native nothingness."

It is learning to "stand still," which seems so difficult for man. I have dealt more fully with this law in the chapter on non-resistance.

I will give another example of sowing and reaping, which came in the most curious way.

A woman came to me saying, she had received a counterfeit twenty-dollar bill, given to her at the bank. She was much disturbed, for, she said, "The people at the bank will never acknowledge their mistake."

I replied, "Let us analyze the situation and find out why you attracted it." She thought a few moments and exclaimed: "I know it, I sent a friend a lot of stagemoney, just for a joke." So the law had sent her some stagemoney, for it doesn't know anything about jokes.

I said, "Now we will call on the law of forgiveness, and neutralize the situation."

Christianity is founded upon the law of forgiveness - Christ has redeemed us from the curse of the Karmic law, and the Christ within each man is his Redeemer and Salvation from all inharmonious conditions.

So I said: "Infinite Spirit, we call on the law of forgiveness and give thanks that she is under grace and not under law, and cannot lose this twenty dollars which is hers by divine right."

"Now," I said, "Go back to the bank and tell them, fearlessly, that it was given you, there by mistake."

She obeyed, and to her surprise, they apologized and gave her another bill, treating her most courteously.

So knowledge of the Law gives man power to "rub out his mistakes." Man cannot force the external to be what he is not.

If he desires riches, he must be rich first in consciousness.

For example: A woman came to me asking treatment for prosperity. She did not take much interest in her household affairs, and her home was in great disorder.

I said to her, "If you wish to be rich, you much be orderly. All men with great wealth are orderly - and order is heaven's first law." I added, "You will never become rich with a burnt match in the pincushion."

She had a good sense of humor and commenced immediately, putting her house in order. She rearranged furniture, straightened out bureau drawers, cleaned rugs, and soon made a big financial demonstration - a gift from a relative. The woman, herself, became made over, and keeps herself keyed-up financially, by being ever watchful of the *external and expecting prosperity, knowing God is her supply.*

Many people are in ignorance of the fact that gifts and things are investments, and that hoarding and saving invariably lead to loss.

"There is that scattereth and yet increaseth; and there is that withholdeth more than is meet, but it tendeth to poverty."

For example: I knew a man who wanted to buy a fur-lined overcoat. He and his wife went to various shops, but there was none he wanted. He said they were all too cheap-looking. At last, he was shown one, the salesman said was valued at a thousand dollars, but which the manager would sell him for five-hundred dollars, as it was late in the season.

His financial possessions amounted to about seven hundred dollars. The reasoning mind would have said, "You can't afford to spend nearly all you have on a coat," but he was very intuitive and never reasoned.

He turned to his wife and said, "If I get this coat, I'll make a ton of money!" So his wife consented, weakly.

About a month later, he received a ten-thousand-dollar commission. The coat made him feel so rich, it linked him with success and prosperity; without the coat he would not have received the commission. It was an investment paying large dividends!

If man ignores these leadings to spend or to give, the same amount of money will go in an uninteresting or unhappy way.

For example: A woman told me, on Thanksgiving Day, she informed her family that they could not afford a Thanksgiving dinner. She had the money, but decided to save it.

A few days later, someone entered her room and took from the bureau drawer the exact amount the dinner would have cost.

The law always stands back of the man who spends fearlessly, with wisdom.

For example: One of my students was shopping with her little nephew. The child clamored for a toy, which she told him she could not afford to buy.

She realized suddenly that she was seeking lack, and not recognizing God as her supply!

So she bought the toy, and on her way home, picked *up, in the street, the exact amount of money she had paid for it.*

Man's supply is inexhaustible and unfailing when fully trusted, but faith or trust must precede the demonstration. "According to your faith be it unto you. ' "Faith is the substance of things hoped for, the evidence of things not seen - " for faith holds the vision steady, and the adverse pictures are dissolved and dissipated, and "in due season we shall reap, if we faint not."

Jesus Christ brought the good news (the gospel) that there was a higher law than the law of Karma - and that that law transcends the law of Karma. It is the law of grace, or forgiveness. It is the law which *frees man from the law of cause and effect - the law of consequence. "Under grace, and not under law."*

We are told that on this plane, man reaps where he has not sown; the gifts of God are simply poured out upon him. "All that the Kingdom affords is his." This continued state of bliss awaits the man who has overcome the race (or world) thought.

In the world thought there is tribulation, but Jesus Christ said: "Be of good cheer; I have overcome the world."

The world thought is that of sin, sickness and death. He saw their absolute unreality and said sickness and sorrow shall pass away and death itself, the last enemy, be overcome.

We know now, from a scientific standpoint, that death could be overcome by stamping the subconscious mind with the conviction of eternal youth and eternal life.

The subconscious, being simply power without direction, *carries out orders without questioning.*

Working under the direction of the superconscious (the Christ or God within man) the "resurrection of the body" would be accomplished.

Man would no longer throw off his body in death, it would be transformed into the "body electric," sung by Walt Whitman, for Christianity is founded upon the forgiveness of sins and "an empty tomb."

Workbook Session Five - The Law of Karma and Law of Forgiveness

In this session:

- The Law of Karma
- Man's Visualization a Manifestation Skill
- Freedom Through Spiritual Law
- Divine Right
- Non-Resistance
- The Law of Forgiveness
- Man's Supply is Inexhaustible/Unfailing
- Overcoming Physical World Conditioning
- Recap and Journal Pages

Begin this session by asking Archangel Michael to surround you with God's Divine White Light of Protection and set your intention to connect with your higher self – the God Part within.

Father, Mother, God, Creator of All That Is…

I claim my personal power and open the way to see clearly my field of potentiality, my field of infinite possibilities. I cut the ties of beliefs and thought patterns that no longer serve me in all directions of time thereby removing them from my consciousness, my subconscious and my superconscious. I fearlessly step into the magnificence of the true essence of who I am – One with God. I graciously accept all that is mine by divine right, under grace in a miraculous way and commit to fulfill all that I came to be, have and do in this incarnation on Mother Earth at this time.

Amen

Ask your guides, angels and teachers to be present with you to help you open your heart, mind and spirit to the infinite possibilities.

All things are possible in God.

THE LAW OF KARMA

Florence explains to us that Karma is the return of man's thoughts, deeds and words. She states that they "return to him sooner or later with astounding accuracy – like boomerangs."

The higher our level of consciousness, the more quickly the energy we put out returns to us. Florence points this out – that knowledge of Spiritual Law is forever – we cannot go back to ignorance – nor would we want to. Working in concert with the three levels of consciousness – bonding with our God Part is our mission – the ultimate goal to accept, understand and practice unconditional love and move into the Fourth Dimensional World of intellectual comprehension.

Sowing good deeds, words and thoughts is most important. For all returns to us – we are the giver and the receiver. God does not punish us – man creates negative or bad things happening to him through negative thought patterns and beliefs – sowing negative or bad seeds.

Do you harbor negative thoughts of others? Thoughts are energy too and will create a good or bad return.

Monitoring our thoughts, words and actions to maintain a foundation of love will make us a magnet for good return. In chapter three, The Power of the Word, Florence taught us that we have the power to neutralize our mistakes by recognizing God as the only power and to call on the Law of Forgiveness.

WORKBOOK ITEM ONE

Look honestly at your life – do you see how you attract/create negative return for yourself? Do you see how you attract/create good/positive return for yourself?

Karma is a little like the Law of Attraction – attracting the degree of energy to you that you put out. Being envious of what another has, blocks you from receiving. Blessing others to have more, opens the door for you to receive. Karma is created in both situations.

In the following form write out several situations where you created bad Karma for yourself. Now write out several situations where you created Good Karma for yourself. Then go back to the Bad Karma and consider ways to change and/or neutralize it. You may discover that there is work to do within to change the behavior or feelings that instigated the bad Karma. Use the tools you've learned to make the change.

Karma Form

Bad Karma:

Good Karma:

Use the Journal Page to write about the behaviors you have discovered in evaluating your creation of bad and good karma. This exercise provides insight into the things we do subconsciously - without thinking. Once we have identified negative thought patterns and/or beliefs, we have the tools to change them and move to a much happier life path.

JOURNAL PAGE:

MAN'S VISUALIZATION A MANIFESTATION SKILL

Many of us live our lives going through the motions of living life. We don't discern what we desire, what we want to do or what we want to accomplish.

Visualization is a powerful manifestation skill. By visualizing we write the record of receipt in our subconscious.

Florence reminds us of this in the examples from previous chapters of the woman who pictured disease manifesting in her child and a woman seeing success for her husband. These things were visualized first – written into the subconscious record and manifested into reality. Notice that one of the examples is negative and one is positive. Coming into knowledge of spiritual law will help us to eliminate manifesting things that are not what we desire.

As children we "make believe" as we play, for we have no limits in imagination. As adults, we must call on these skills of unrestricted, clear thinking to reach deep within us to discern what we truly desire – what is ours by divine right – what is ours in our Field of Potentiality. God has great abundance for us – it is we, who must understand how limitless we truly are to receive.

In getting our minds around and flexing our ability to visualize what we want to receive, what we want to do, what we want to be, or what we want to accomplish, we find ourselves truly limitless. In God all things are possible.

WORKBOOK ITEM TWO

Determine one thing that you desire. Write what it is under Thank You, God, for: column. Can you visualize receiving it? Can you reach a feeling of elation of opulence due to having received? Write about it under Visualize Receipt column.

Visualization

Thank You, God, for:	Visualize Receipt

Use the Journal Page to write about your discoveries. Is it easy or difficult for you to discern what you desire? Is it easy or difficult for you to visualize? If it is difficult, why? Do you have lingering feelings of unworthiness? Use your tools to be rid of unworthy feelings.

JOURNAL PAGE:

FREEDOM THROUGH SPIRITUAL LAW

Spiritual, Universal laws affect us whether we know about them or not. Understanding and implementing Spiritual/Universal Law into our daily lives in positive, love based ways, frees us from the conditioning of the physical world – from mortal thought – from fear. As we apply spiritual laws in love based format, into the moments of our days we bring into concert the three levels of consciousness. They work together as one, bringing balance, peace and love to our lives. Our bond with God becomes strong and we come to accept it as a natural part of our lives – like breathing. The trust and faith become part of us instead of something we have to work at continually. We become one with God The Father.

In becoming One with God, we find ourselves free of physical world stress and worry – of fear. We are free to follow through on our Divine Life Path sharing the grace and love of God with all we meet. We become miracle magnets for all the abundance God has for us. As we mentioned before, receiving good things is not a reward for good behavior, it is our birthright.

WORKBOOK ITEM THREE

This exercise is designed to show you your spiritual growth since opening this workbook. Sit quietly and read through the form. Evaluate your life honestly. Under the Before column briefly write out what your life was like before you began this work. Then under the Now column write what your life is like now.

Spiritual Growth Square of Life Form

Before	Now
Health	Health

Wealth	Wealth
Love	Love
Work	Work

Use the Journal Pages to write about your evaluation. Write about the things you've discovered about yourself – your connection with God, with others and the blessings that have come into your life. Also write about how you "see" God around you.

JOURNAL PAGE:

DIVINE RIGHT

Florence tells us that "the divine pattern is the only safe pattern to work by. Desire is a tremendous force, and must be directed in the right channels, or chaos ensues." She is trying to help us understand how to ask "aright."

In visualizing something that isn't ours by divine right, we run the risk of manifesting disaster or chaos into our lives. We will receive because we become a magnet for what we desire through visualization and gratitude of receipt, even though it is not for our highest good. Florence uses the example of the woman who wanted a specific house – not the house that was hers by divine right, but someone else's house. She got what she asked for, but did not find happiness in the ownership.

How do we know that what we want is ours and will bring harmony and happiness or that it belongs to someone else and will bring disaster and/or chaos to our lives? Evaluate your Sponsoring Thought. How does it feel within you? Is it fear based, or love based?

When we order something to come to us by divine right, we are ordering what is ours from a basis of love. If we demand/order what someone else has, we are coveting what they have – this is an order to the universe from a negative, fear basis.

We each have our own Field of Potentiality – things that are ours by Divine Right – perfect health, wealth, love and self-expression (work) plus material things. If we can dream it, it is in our Field of Potentiality. It is crucial that we set our intention to receive that which we desire for it is ours by Divine Right. Throwing feelings of unworthiness into the mix opens the way to manifesting that which is not in our Field of Potentiality, hence it is not ours by Divine right and leaves us unfulfilled.

We must be specific in putting in an order with God – we must order (demand/command) what is ours from a basis of love – from our Field of Potentiality - **"by divine right."**

God has great abundance for us – for each one of us. We have "free will" in not only what we ask for, but how we ask for it. When we ask for things to come to us by divine right and under grace, in a perfect way, we "cover the ground" and ask God to send to us our highest good. In receiving our highest good, we often receive even better than what we asked for.

Florence points out that "anything forced into manifestation through personal will is always 'ill-got' and has 'ever bad success'." "Faith is the substance of things hoped for, the evidence of things not seen – for faith holds the vision steady, and the adverse pictures are dissolved and dissipated."

Jesus taught that what we pray for has already been accomplished. When we give God direction for what we want to manifest in our lives, it is then time to graciously thank him as if we have already received – writing our subconscious record and opening the doors to receive.

Receiving isn't about asking God for things – it is all about thanking God for receipt: "Thank you, God for sending to me ___(fill in the blank)___ by divine right, under grace in a perfect way," and trusting that the order will be fulfilled.

WORKBOOK ITEM FOUR

This exercise is designed to help you place an order with the Universal Supply Warehouse.

NOTE: We live in an abundant universe. The universe does not care whether we want a glass of water because we're thirsty or a new house because we're being evicted from the old one. It simply matches to us that which we focus/desire. This is why it is SO important that we discern what we desire and request. We receive it by Divine Right under grace in a wonderful way.

Universal Supply Warehouse Order Form

1. Ask/Discern what you truly desire.
2. Fill in the form
3. Believe/Let it Happen/Attitude of Gratitude/Visualize Receipt in Gratitude
4. Receive/Gratitude

Receipt Action: Be open to guidance of action to take (if any) to receive desire.

Delivery Details: As designed by God under grace by divine right in a perfect way.

UNIVERSAL SUPPLY WAREHOUSE ORDER FORM

Description of Desire	Price
	By Divine Right
Shipping & Handling: Under Grace in a Wonderful Way	

Did you find yourself feeling confident as you filled out the form? Or did you feel skeptical or unworthy? If your order does not resonate with you, look within to discern why. You may use the Healing Circle of Love on page 279 to discern if your order is in your Field of Potential or if something better is. The Healing Circle of Love will also reveal to you any layers of fear that you may need to dissipate.

Use the Journal Page to write about your experience in discerning and ordering from the universe what you truly desire.

JOURNAL PAGE:

NON-RESISTANCE

Man has a hard time relinquishing control of people, situations and conditions. We want to control everything. In executing control over all that we face in our lives, we effectively block the abundance and the help of God. Man's will is done – not God's.

In relinquishing this need to control, man becomes non-resistant and draws to him what he asks for.

Florence uses the example of the woman whose daughter wanted to take a trip that would be hazardous. The woman forced her personal will on the daughter and forbade her to go through fear. The fear acted as a magnet and made the trip more attractive to the daughter. Florence told her: "Let go, and take your mental hands off; put it in God's Hands, and use this statement: I put this situation in the hands of Infinite Love and Wisdom; if this trip is the Divine plan, I bless it and no longer resist, but if it is not divinely planned, I give thanks that it is now dissolved and dissipated."

Let's evaluate this. The affirmation blessed the situation (we've learned how powerful blessing a person and/or situation is) and she gave thanks for the plans being dissolved even though there was no dissolving in site.

The words transmuted the woman's fear to feelings of love based non-resistance, thereby, dissipating the fear. The magnetic pull of the fear vanished.

The three levels of consciousness were working in tandem once again. The conscious mind stated the affirmation. The superconscious mind trusted God to handle the situation and the subconscious mind's record was rewritten from one of fear, to one of non-resistance and trust shifted the mom to a state of love.

WORKBOOK ITEM FIVE

This exercise is designed to evaluate your ability to use your free will wisely by working in tandem with God – practicing non-resistance.

Review the form. In the Situation/Event columns write in a situation/event that has taken place before and since you've been working in this workbook. Evaluate your actions. Did you work with God and allow His will to be done or did you try to handle everything on your own? What was the end result? Write your actions in the appropriate column.

BEFORE AND AFTER RESULTS

Situation/Event before experiencing this workbook
My Reaction
Situation/Event after experiencing this workbook
My Reaction

Use the Journal Page to write about your discoveries. What happened before you had the tools in the workbook? How did you implement your tools to achieve non-resistance? Are you seeing that everything you do is a choice? Are you understanding the power of non-resistance?

JOURNAL PAGE

THE LAW OF FORGIVENESS

"Jesus Christ taught that there was a higher law than the law of Karma – and that that law transcends the law of Karma. It is the law of grace or forgiveness. It is the law which frees man from the law of cause and effect – the law of consequence. Under grace, and not under law."

Florence states that "Christ has redeemed us from the curse of the Karmic law, and the Christ within each man is his Redeemer and Salvation from all inharmonious conditions."

Through the Law of Attraction we become magnetized to the energy frequencies we put out to the Universe. If our energy is negative, we become a magnet for same – bad karma. If we transmute our negativity to a basis of love, we become a magnet for same – good Karma.

In the example of the woman who created negative Karma for herself through giving someone counterfeit money as a joke. The Universe has no sense of humor, nor does the subconscious mind, as we have learned. The subconscious mind writes records to manifest things into our lives – it does not know that the woman was joking about counterfeit money.

By asking forgiveness of God, then practicing active faith and trust that we are forgiven our subconscious record is rewritten, effectively stopping the negative from manifesting. The negative is replaced with love and harmony, making us a magnet for only love – fear is eradicated.

When we forgive others, we transmute our feelings from feelings based in fear to feelings based in love. This raises our vibrational frequency of energy to love, effectively notifying the Universal Supply Warehouse to "match" love based people, things and situations to us.

When we forgive ourselves, we transmute more feelings from fear to love – remember EVERYTHING is either love based or fear based – there is no in between. After forgiving ourselves, our energy frequency is raised to an even higher vibration to attract even higher abundance.

WORKBOOK ITEM SIX

This exercise is designed to help you forgive – raising your vibrational frequency making you a magnet for higher vibrational desires. Look honestly at your life. Write about an event/person you need to forgive under the Situation/Event/Relationship column. You may use the Healing Circle of Love or Sedona Method of Release or other tools to forgive. Write about the experience in the Forgiveness Experience column.

Forgiveness Form

Situation/Event/Relationship	Forgiveness Experience

Use the Journal Page to write about what you discovered about yourself in this exercise. Were you able to forgive? Or do you still have that "angst" feeling in your chest or belly? Forgive yourself for your part in the event. Write about your experience.

JOURNAL PAGE:

MAN'S SUPPLY IS INEXHAUSTIBLE/UNFAILING

God is the true one and only power.

God is limitless. His supply of abundance is inexhaustible and unfailing. God is the Universal Supply Warehouse.

We are limitless spiritual beings experiencing a human existence. As humans we limit ourselves through physical world conditioning often times dissolving our dreams completely. Through this conditioning we also come to the belief that we are unworthy to receive good things.

When we work together with the God Part within, we effectively dissipate these self imposed limits both on ourselves and on God. We work together as one practicing trust and faith that God is our supply. It is through this partnership that we change our way of thinking – we rewrite our subconscious records to reflect the limitlessness of God and ourselves. In conjunction with the tools we are learning we achieve the feelings of opulence and expect prosperity – because we are prosperous from within. What is written in the subconscious mind within, manifests to the external – it is Universal Law.

As humans we have a tendency to be fearful of letting go of money – we do not trust God as our supply. Florence shares the example of the woman who told her family they could not afford a Thanksgiving dinner, then someone stole from her what the dinner would have cost. She was fearful of letting go of the money and the fear became as a magnet and drew to her a thief. Another example Florence shares is of the woman who boldly cast fear of lack aside and purchased a toy for a child - claiming God as her supply. She later found the exact amount she paid for the toy in the street – she trusted in God as her supply and she received.

The two women were magnets for what they felt in their hearts – one was fear based – one was love based.

WORKBOOK ITEM SEVEN

A. This exercise is designed to evaluate your thought patterns of your square of life. We will discern love base or fear base. Read each section and evaluate your innermost feelings. When you read each section, do you feel joyful and abundant? Write your feelings in the space. If there is a section that does NOT feel joyful and abundant, how does it feel and why? Look within for what is holding back joy – where is the fear? Remember if it isn't love based – joy, then it is fear based. Use your tools to dissipate the fear.

Remember, you are living a human experience – daily you are bombarded with fear and negativity. Fear will sneak back into your thoughts and feelings. Identify it and use your tools to dissipate it.

Our Square of Life Today Form

Health – A healthy physical body that houses our spirit

Love - Relationships that are fulfilling and love based

Perfect Self-Expression – Work that fulfills our passion that we love

Wealth – Cash flow that fulfills our needs and desires

B. Read through the form once you've completed it and evaluate each area of the square of your life. When you review each one, do you feel complete peace, contentment and love? If not, evaluate why. Is there something you can change within you to make it better? If so, what is it and what tool can you use to make the change?

Use The Sedona Method® of Release or the Healing Circle of Love to dissipate fear and shift you to a source of love.

Use the Journal Page to write about your internal progress. Do you feel lighter? Freer? Happier? More as One with God?

These evaluations are necessary to prevent us from becoming stagnant in our spiritual growth. We are also growing stronger – being able to maintain our connection with God no matter how negative or chaotic the physical world is around us. Our quality of life has improved dramatically thereby, touching all who are around us in beautiful, loving ways.

JOURNAL PAGE:

OVERCOMING PHYSICAL WORLD CONDITIONING

"Jesus Christ said: Be of good cheer; I have overcome the world." Jesus understood that the spirit lives forever, that only the physical body dies.

The physical world teaches that death is something to be feared, when in truth death is but a breath of transition from the physical world to the spiritual. Death is not to be feared, but to be honored.

Florence states that a "continued state of bliss awaits the man who has overcome the race (or world) thought." We've learned that this is true. We have learned through the workbook exercises that the teaching of the physical world, the conditioning, is a false power that is limited, negative and destructive. The conditioning is a block between us and God.

We've learned tools to overcome physical world conditioning. What we must understand is that we are still spirits experiencing a human existence. As humans we are susceptible to the conditioning of the physical world. It is up to us to daily monitor the affect the world has on our collective consciousness. It is up to us to use the tools we've learned to eradicate any negativity that is revealed to us or has made its way into our thought patterns or beliefs. In shaking off the physical world principles daily we are able to maintain our spiritual balance of the three levels of consciousness. Stress worry and fear become a thing of the past and profound, prosperous abundance in the square of life becomes our daily routine instead of a wish. We become a magnet for miracles.

RECAP

This Chapter of Law and Unforgiveness helps us to become more aware of the cause and effect of our deeds, words and thoughts. Our understanding becomes more complete about Karma and how to neutralize what we unintentionally set into motion with the energy of our words and thoughts. We recognize now how visualization skills write our subconscious records and how to use that tool for our highest good.

By journaling and using the workbook items we now know how to use the Universal Laws in a positive manner to bring to us what we desire instead of what we don't desire.

Deep within us we are becoming accustomed to the fact that God is our supply and that we are worthy of abundance. Physical world conditioning does not stop over night. In addition, we are reintroduced to it on a daily basis by interacting with the outside world in the form of internet, phone, television, radio, etc. It is important that we monitor our words, thoughts and deeds on a moment to moment basis during our daily lives in order to break the cycle. Maintaining a lifestyle free from negativity takes patience and diligence – yet the rewards are beyond measure. Practicing living from a foundation of love and working in tandem with the three levels of consciousness in balance are the keys to a fulfilled square of life.

Honor those around you. Honor yourself. Honor God. Allow the God Part within to come out to play. Allow the God Part within to help you make decisions. Acknowledge the blessings that come to your life – graciously give thanks. Use the Journal Pages to write about the changes you are experiencing in your life. The more you allow yourself to have "the eyes to see," the more you *will* see!

Be sure to thank your guides, teachers and angels for being in attendance and helping you to clearly understand God's work.

May you be profoundly blessed in this moment and in every moment after...

JOURNAL PAGES:

JOURNAL PAGES continued:

When man knows his own powers and the workings of his mind, his great desire is to find an easy and quick way to impress the subconscious with good, for simply an intellectual knowledge of the Truth will not bring results.

In my own case, I found the easiest way is in "casting the burden."

A metaphysician once explained it in this manner. He said, "The only thing which gives anything weight in nature, is the law of gravitation, and if a boulder could be taken high above the planet, there would be no weight in that boulder; and that is what Jesus Christ meant when he said: "My yoke is easy and my burden is light."

He had overcome the world vibration, and functioned in the fourth dimensional realm, where there is only perfection, completion, life and joy.

He said: "Come to me all ye that are labor and are heavy laden, and I will give you rest." "Take my yoke upon you, for my yoke is easy and my burden is light."

We are also told in the fifty-fifth Psalm, to "cast thy burden upon the Lord." Many passages in the Bible state that the *battle is God's* not man's and that man is always to *"stand still" and see the Salvation of the Lord.*

This indicates that the superconscious mind (or Christ within) is the department which fights man's battle and relieves him of burdens.

We see, therefore, that man violates law if he carries a burden, and a burden is an adverse thought or condition, and this thought or condition has its root in the subconscious.

It seems almost impossible to make any headway directing the subconscious from the conscious or reasoning mind, as the reasoning mind (the intellect) is limited in its conceptions, and filled with doubts and fears.

How scientific it then is, to cast the burden upon the superconscious mind (or Christ within) where it is "made light," or dissolved into its native nothingness."

For example: A woman in urgent need of money, "made light" upon the Christ within, the superconscious, with the statement, "I cast this burden of lack on the Christ (within) and I go free to have plenty!"

The belief in lack was her burden, and as she cast it upon the Superconscious with its belief of plenty, an avalanche of supply was the result.

We read, "The Christ in you the hope of glory."

Another example: One of my students had been given a new piano, and there was no room in her studio for it until she had moved out the old one. She was in a state of perplexity. She wanted to keep the old piano, but knew of no place to send it. She became desperate, as the new piano was to be sent immediately; in fact, was on its way, with no place to put it. She said it came to her to repeat, "I cast this burden on the Christ within, and I go free."

A few moments later, her 'phone rang, and a woman friend asked if she might rent her old piano, and it was moved out, a few minutes before the new one arrived.

I knew a woman, whose burden was resentment. She said, "I cast this burden of resentment on the Christ within, and I go free, to be loving, harmonious and happy." The Almighty superconscious, flooded the subconscious with love, and her whole life was changed. For years, resentment had held her in a state of torment and imprisoned her soul (the subconscious mind).

The statement should be made over and over and over, sometimes for hours at a time, silently or audibly, with quietness but determination.

I have often compared it to winding-up a victrola. We must wind ourselves up with spoken words.

I have noticed, in "casting the burden," after a little while, one seems to see clearly. It is impossible to have clear vision, while in the throes of carnal mind. Doubts and fear poison the mind and body and imagination runs riot, attracting disaster and disease.

In steadily repeating the affirmation, "I cast this burden on the Christ within, and go free," the vision clears, and with it a feeling of relief, and sooner or later comes *the manifestation of good, be it health, happiness or supply.*

One of my students once asked me to explain the "darkness before the dawn." I referred in a preceding chapter to the fact that often, before the big demonstration "everything seems to go wrong," and deep depression clouds the consciousness. It means that out of the subconscious are rising the doubts and fears of the ages. These old derelicts of the subconscious rise to the surface, *to be put out.*

It is then that man should clap his cymbals, like Jehoshaphat, and give thanks that he is saved, even though he seems surrounded by the enemy (the situation of lack or disease). The student continued, "How long must one remain in the dark" and I replied, "until one *can see in the dark*, and *"casting the burden enables one to see in the dark."*

In order to impress the subconscious, active faith is always essential.

"Faith without works is dead." In these chapters I have endeavored to bring out this point.

Jesus Christ showed active faith when "He commanded the multitude to sit down on the ground," before he gave thanks for the loaves and fishes.

I will give another example showing how necessary this step is. In fact, active faith is the bridge, over which man passes to his Promised Land.

Through misunderstanding, a woman had been separated from her husband, whom she loved deeply. He refused all offers of reconciliation and would not communicate with her in any way.

Coming into the knowledge of Spiritual law, she denied the appearance of separation. She made this statement:

"There is no separation in Divine Mind, therefore, I cannot be separated form the love and companionship which are mine by divine right."

She showed active faith by arranging a place for him at the table every day; thereby impressing the subconscious with a picture of his return. Over a year passed, but she never wavered, and one day he walked in.

The subconscious is often impressed through music. Music has a fourth dimensional quality and releases the soul from imprisonment. It makes wonderful things seem *possible, and easy of accomplishment!*

I have a friend who uses her victrola, daily, for this purpose. It puts her in perfect harmony and releases the imagination.

Another woman often dances while making her affirmations. The rhythm and harmony of music and motion carry her words forth with tremendous power.

The student must remember also, not to despise the "day of small things."

Invariably, before a demonstration, come "signs of land."

Before Columbus reached America, he saw birds and twigs which showed him land was near. So it is with a demonstration; but often the student mistakes it for the demonstration itself, and is disappointed.

For example: A woman had "spoken the word" for a set of dishes. Not long afterwards a friend gave her a dish which was old and cracked.

She came to me and said, "Well, I asked for a set of dishes, and all I got was a cracked plate."

I replied, "The plate was only signs of land. It shows your dishes are coming - look upon it as a birds and seaweed," and not long afterwards the dishes came.

Continually "making-believe," impresses the subconscious. If one makes believe he is rich, and makes believe he is successful, in "due time he will reap."

Children are always "making believe," and "except ye be converted, and become as little children, ye shall not enter the Kingdom of Heaven."

For example: I know of a woman who was very poor, but no one could make her feel poor. She earned a small amount of money from rich friends, who constantly reminded her of her poverty, and to be careful and saving.

Regardless of their admonitions, she would spend all her earnings on a hat, or make someone a gift, and be in a rapturous state of mind. Her thoughts were always centered on beautiful clothes and "rings and things," but without envying others.

She lived in the world of the wondrous, and only riches seemed real to her. Before long she married a rich man, and the rings and things became visible. I do not know whether the man was the "Divine Selection," but opulence had to manifest in her life, as she had imaged only opulence.

There is no peace or happiness for man, until he has erased all fear from the subconscious.

Fear is misdirected energy and must be redirected, or transmuted into Faith.

Jesus Christ said, "Why are ye fearful, O ye of little faith?" "All things are possible to him that believeth."

I am asked, so often by my students, "How can I get rid of fear?"

I reply, "By walking up to the thing you are afraid of."

"The lion takes its fierceness from your fear."

Walk up to the lion, and he will disappear; run away and he runs after you.

I have shown in previous chapters, how the lion of lack disappeared when the individual spent money farlessly, showing faith that God was his supply and therefore, unfailing.

Many of my students have come out of the bondage of poverty, and are now bountifully supplied, through losing all fear of letting money go out. The subconscious is impressed with the truth that *God is the Giver and Gift*; therefore as one is one with the Giver, he is one with the Gift. A splendid statement is, "I now thank God the Giver for God the Gift."

Man has so long separated himself from his good and his supply, through thoughts of separation and lack, that sometimes, it takes dynamite to dislodge these false ideas from the subconscious, and the dynamite is a big situation.

We see in the foregoing illustration, how the individual was freed from his bondage by *showing fearlessness.*

154

Man should watch himself hourly to detect if his motive for action is fear or faith.

"Choose ye this day whom we shall serve," fear or faith.

Perhaps one's fear is of personality. Then do not avoid the people feared; be willing to meet them cheerfully, and they will either prove "golden links in the chain of one's good," or disappear harmoniously from one's pathway.

Perhaps one's fear is of disease or germs. Then one should be fearless and undisturbed in a germ-laden situation, and he would be immune.

One can only contract germs while vibrating at the same rate as the germ, and fear drags men down to the level of the germ. Of course, the disease laden germ is the product of carnal mind, as all thought must objectify.

Germs do not exist in the superconscious or Divine Mind, therefore are the product of man's "vain imagination."

"In the twinkling of an eye," man's release will come when he realizes *there is no power in evil.*

The material world will fade away, and the fourth dimensional world, the "World of the Wondrous," will swing into manifestation.

"And I saw a new heaven, and a new earth - and there shall be no more death, neither sorrow nor crying, neither shall there be any more pain; for the former things are passed away."

Workbook Session Six - Casting the Burden

In this session:

- Casting the Burden
- Darkness Before the Dawn
- Active Faith and Anchoring
- Island Before Paradise
- Making Believe/Visualization to Anchor Dreams
- Fear
- God is the Giver & the Receiver
- The Fourth Dimensional World
- Recap and Journal Pages

Begin this session by asking Archangel Michael to surround you with God's Divine White Light of Protection and set your intention to connect with your higher self – the God Part within.

Father, Mother, God, Creator of All That Is…

I claim my personal power and open the way to see clearly my field of potentiality, my field of infinite possibilities. I cut the ties of beliefs and thought patterns that no longer serve me in all directions of time thereby removing them from my consciousness, my subconscious and my superconscious. I fearlessly step into the magnificence of the true essence of who I am – One with God. I graciously accept all that is mine by divine right, under grace in a miraculous way and commit to fulfill all that I came to be, have and do in this incarnation on Mother Earth at this time.

Amen

Ask your guides, angels and teachers to be present with you to help you open your heart, mind and spirit to the infinite possibilities.

In God's world, the fourth dimensional world of Divine Mind,
there is no death, no disease, no sorrow – only perfection,
completion, life and joy – love. Man <u>can</u> attain this!

CASTING THE BURDEN

Florence states that man violates spiritual law if he carries a burden. He violates the law because he puts his fears and worries – his burdens – above the power of God. To give all our worries, our fears – our burdens, to God requires complete Trust that God, can handle them – that He is our supply in all things. In order to completely trust in God, man must release his desire to control.

The physical world is all about burden. We worry, we fret, we fear – and we're taught that these are the side affects of living a responsible life. Man's idea of living a responsible life is to be in control. When man feels the need to control, he is living from a source of fear – separate from God. If we aren't working with God, then we're working with the physical world and the physical world is fear, worry, limiting ourselves, resentment, lack, and judgment – burdens. We're taught to be responsible – trusting in God to care for us – giving our control to Him to be our supply, is this responsible behavior?

It is the ONLY responsible behavior.

What *IS* our responsibility here in the physical world? The angels will tell us our mission is LOVE. We can't love fully and completely when fear is involved. Fear overshadows love and takes on a life of its own. Fear takes control. This means that instead of love being the source of our lives, fear is in control.

The God Part within us is love - always there, no matter what we do, no matter what we think or say – God is always with us – within us to help us – loving us unconditionally and without judgment. It is up to us to take our power back from physical world conditioning – fear based living – use our free will wisely and ask God to help us. It is up to us to allow God to take our burdens, so we may go about our lives freely to share our prosperous abundance with others, thereby; passing forward God's love.

So in order to cast all our burdens aside and live free in the palm of the hand of God we must rid ourselves of mortal thought – of physical world conditioning. We must raise our level of consciousness to that of the fourth dimensional realm.

And how do we do this? How do we cast our burdens, our fears?

To rid ourselves of our fears, no matter what they are, we must tap into the universal wisdom of God. For within the palm of God is safety. We humans seek safety – in tapping into the life line of God we will be able to release the hold we have on the familiar – fear and doubt. It is very sad that fear and doubt become normal and familiar – like breathing – but it is true. In setting the intention and making our connection with God, we open the door to allow ourselves to feel the love of God – to experience the all encompassing comfort and safety of His profound love. It is at this time that our vibratory level will elevate and we will be able to grasp the concept of life without doubt and fear.

In practicing our releasing methods we will get a glimpse of the Fourth Dimensional World – free of fear, judgment, and lack. Through this glimpse we will have the strength and desire to complete the releasing of all our burdens – all our fears and doubts. It is now that we truly *feel* the love of God within – we feel all the way to our essence that we are worthy to receive God's abundance – all traces of fear and doubt – our burdens are gone! When we breathe deeply we *feel within…* the elation of opulence!

WORKBOOK ITEM ONE:

In previous exercises you've looked within and found fear. You defined what you were afraid of and taken the appropriate steps to release that fear from within. As mentioned before, we are as an onion – as we evolve, more layers of fear are revealed to us. Plus by being in contact with negativity left and right through simply living, unintentionally some of the fear has crept back in.

This happens because even though you are a spiritual being, you are having a human experience. As a human, negativity and conditioning of the physical world does impact you. You focus on working with God, but in going about your daily life in the physical world of Earth, negativity does influence you and it can resurrect feelings of fear and doubt.

When you think about the things that worry you the most you feel it in your body. It is real and it is there – giving you that "angst" feeling in your chest or your belly. Again, identify what they are and where they are. They may be somewhat different than the last time we looked.

Looking within to identify burdens:

As you read the sections of the Square of Life Form, review/examine the emotions that are generated by each section. Do this HONESTLY! Do you feel anxious in an area, fearful, joyful, and/or confident? What are the burdens hiding behind false confidence? Write down your feelings as you go through the form.

Before you begin, sit quietly and breathe deeply. Ask your angels to reveal to you what you need to work on to move more fully into stepping into your power and receiving your highest good.

Square of Life Form

Health - A healthy physical body that houses our spirit
Love - Relationships that are fulfilling and love based
Perfect Self-Expression – Work that fulfills our passion that we love
Wealth – Cash flow that fulfills our needs and desires

With each session of this workbook, you become more open to the All of God. You become more "in tune" with your own thoughts, emotions and deep seated beliefs. With each session you strip away layer after layer of physical world conditioning.

Where you surprised at what you found when you looked honestly at your life? Now that the burdens have been identified, use the Healing Circle of Love or The Sedona Method® of Release to dissipate them and shift to a source of love. Use the Journal Page to write about your discoveries.

In asking God to take your fears, in casting your burden, and truly giving them to Him – whatever they are, you free yourself to do your best in everything else. You free yourself of worrying about the mortgage so you can pass on God's love to others. When you are worried, doubtful and fearful, you're not at your best – you are preoccupied.

Ask God to make your life easier… He will.

JOURNAL PAGE:

DARKNESS BEFORE THE DAWN

Each time we incarnate to planet earth we bring with us experiences of past lives – both good and bad. We bring forward with us all the love we have given and received as well as any burdens we are still clinging to. We bring forth the level of consciousness that we were experiencing from previous lives.

As humans who take in daily the negativities of the physical world, it becomes a challenge to hold fast to our faith in God as our supply. We have years of experience that doubt and fear are normal. Florence talks about asking God for something, then trusting with faith that God will provide it. We try to do this, but often times we get anxious to receive and doubt begins to creep in. This is when all the burdens of fear that we have not cast out, both in previous lives and in the current one, take hold of our faith and shakes it – the darkness before the dawn.

The darkness before the dawn is man's way of testing his faith and trust in God. We decide whether we allow doubt and fear to override faith and trust – we decide!

Those who are strong in faith and trust in God - knowing within that we *will* receive – are not taken in by these doubts and fear. When we feel the fear rising within us it is then that we must embrace the doubts and fears to us, thereby; dissipating them into our one-ness with God. The Sedona Method® of release and the Healing Circle of Love tools teaches us this. We've also learned to *bless adversity*, "Darkness before the Dawn."

Those of us who don't know how to do this, those who do not have a releasing tool, tend to ask for something, and then negate the receipt of it. We plan what we'll do when we *don't* receive what we've asked for and we effectively "Block" our good from coming to us.

By casting the burden, releasing our fear and replacing the fear with love, the darkness will dissipate and we become a magnet for our highest good – that for which we desire.

WORKBOOK ITEM TWO:

Review past situations of faith and trust, of asking and receiving or effectively blocking receipt. Through this exercise learn will learn how to recognize self sabotage of allowing doubts and fears to control you.

Think about something you have asked God for both prior to experiencing this workbook and since. Write it down under "I asked God for this:" Then evaluate what happened and write it down under the appropriate column.

Faith and Trust Form

I asked God for this:	
What happened?	
I followed through with Faith and Trust	I allowed Fear and Doubt to take over

Use the Journal Page to write about your experience identifying your turning points - when you chose to have faith and to trust or when you chose to negate receipt with fear and doubt. If you have trouble with a past issue – use a current one – ask God for something and write about your experience. Be honest concerning holding to faith and trust or allowing fear and doubt to take over.

JOURNAL PAGE:

ACTIVE FAITH AND ANCHORING

Active faith is putting our feelings of gratitude within into action for what we have asked for when there is no sign of it in site. We've discussed this before, but as humans, getting our mind around this can be challenging, because it goes against physical world teachings and conditioning.

Active faith anchors belief of receiving in the universe. Anchoring it in the universe writes the CD of our subconscious as if we have received – then the subconscious works behind the scenes manifesting the item or event into our world.

When we go into a restaurant and place our order, we don't go into the kitchen to make sure the cook or chef prepares what we ordered. Instead we sit at our table preparing to receive our food. Sometimes we can even taste it - this is definitely showing active faith and experiential visualization!

There are unlimited ways to anchor our requests. These are but a few:

- write them down in a journal or put them in a prayer box
- affirming receipt through affirmations
- purchasing something in preparation of receiving
- visualizing receipt
- celebrating receipt
- making believe (see below)

A Powerful Anchoring Tool: The Four Fundamentals

In the book *"Angelspeake How to Talk With Your Angels"* by Barbara Mark and Trudy Griswold we learn of the Four Fundamentals. They are keys to manifesting the life you desire – implementing The Law of Attraction on your behalf are:

1. Ask/Discern/Demand
2. Believe
3. Let it Happen
4. Say Thank You/Gratitude/Receive

Ask/Discern/Demand: Asking for what you want puts you in a state of lack because you are in a state of 'wanting" - you don't have what you're asking for.

The Bible tells us, "Ask and ye shall receive." Florence uses the word "demand." Demanding of God doesn't quite sound right – it sounds harsh, abrasive and perhaps a little arrogant, but when we go to the dictionary, it states Demand is: "to claim formally." "To claim formally" doesn't have such a critical connotation; instead the reality is that demanding what we desire is actually a love based action. (There will be more about "demanding" what we desire in Chapter 8.)

Ask is discernment - begin by discerning what it is that you desire. Once you have decided, then you may demand/place your order with the Supply Warehouse – God/The Universe. Create your Sponsoring Thought – visualize – make believe you have what you desire – this places your order. You don't need to repeat it over and over – just maintain it. Maintain your Sponsoring Thought – what you desire in the love base it was created by not allowing doubt or fear to interfere with it.

Maintaining an Attitude of Gratitude for what we desire makes us a magnet for what we desire. If you begin to waiver – begin to doubt – revisit visualizing having received and again achieve the Attitude of Gratitude.

It is imperative to be clear with your order. If you are unclear or mixed in what you desire, then The Universe will bring to you mixed people, situations or things. Be – clear – with – your - order. If you order a cheeseburger with the works at a restaurant, but you don't want onions on it, you must tell the wait person or you will get onions. Be specific when you place your order at the Supply Warehouse of the Universe.

Believe/Let it Happen: Visualize and make believe what it would feel like to have received your desire. Once you've achieved the feeling of experiencing your order through visualization and make believe, it's easier to believe it is possible to receive.

Don't worry about HOW God/The Universe will bring to fruition your desire. How it happens isn't your job. The Law of Attraction teaches us the Universe works behind the scenes matching up levels of energetic vibrations. Trying to work out "how" it will happen is showing doubt – doubt is a fear based thought pattern and will negate your receipt.

However, you may be guided to an inspired action to bring about receipt. Be mindful that the action will be effortless and natural – if you struggle, then step back and determine if you've allowed fear in. Visualize yourself into the feelings of opulence and receipt. The desire to continue with the action you were struggling with will either dissipate or it will become clear what to do – then step into the action!

Say Thank you/Receive/Gratitude: Gratitude of receiving sets the intent of having received. To be in a state of gratitude maintains the frequency level of energy. The Universe is able to "match" to us that which we desire.

You are already implementing The Law of Attraction in your life. It is up to you as to whether you consciously attract the life you want or you allow your unsupervised thoughts and beliefs to create your life – in all probability a life you don't want.

For more information on The Four Fundamentals, please pick up your copy of Angelspeake How to Talk With Your Angels by Barbara Mark and Trudy Griswold.

ISLAND BEFORE PARADISE

In practicing active faith of receiving God's bounty we will receive signs from God that our abundance is on its way. Florence explains how this works with the example of the woman who asked for new dishes and received a cracked plate. The cracked plate was a sign from God not to waiver; that what she had asked for was on the way!

Receiving signs can be tricky. Receipt of a sign is the signal to graciously acknowledge receipt but often times we receive the sign and, like the woman and the cracked plate, are disappointed that we did not receive what we asked for. In holding on to this mind set we will effectively "block" our receipt of the paradise.

We have the choice of continuing to actively have faith in receiving or negating through disappointment and blocking receipt. This is also an example of Darkness Before the Dawn – do we allow doubt and fear to take hold of us or do we celebrate faith, trust and gratitude of receipt?

This is the time to *bless* the sign sincerely and claim what we've ordered from the Universal Supply Warehouse as Success and fully received!

MAKING BELIEVE/VISUALIZATION TO ANCHOR DREAMS

Florence quotes "except ye be converted, and become as little children, ye shall not enter the Kingdom of Heaven."

As children playing make believe, there is no fear or doubt – so there is no fear based energy in the subconscious to block receipt. Making believe writes the CD of our subconscious – it is a way of anchoring what we desire into the universe.

* In Make Believe anything is possible.

* In Make Believe, we allow ourselves to dream big, because there are no limits.

* In Make Believe we focus only on what is positive and good – we don't focus on negative, fearful things.

What would you dream of in Make Believe? When you think of this, does anything come to mind or has the limited physical world conditioning eradicated all your dreams?

Spend at least fifteen minutes in Make Believe – as if you were a child. What will you focus on?

WORKBOOK ITEM FOUR:

Sit quietly and think about your square of life. Take one section at a time and Make Believe about something you would like to receive. Write it down under the appropriate heading.

Square of Life Make Believe/Visualization Form

Health – A healthy physical body that houses our spirit
Love - Relationships that are fulfilling and love based
Perfect Self-Expression – Work that fulfills our passion that we love

Wealth – Cash flow that fulfills our needs and desires

NOTE: If you can dream of the desires you wrote about in the Make Believe/Visualization From, the source of your dreams is IN your Field of Potentiality!

Use the Journal Page to write about your discoveries! Did your creativity begin to flow? Did your heart leap with the joy at the realization of the true limitlessness and possibilities of dreams long forgotten?

JOURNAL PAGE:

FEAR

Jesus Christ said, "Why are ye fearful, O ye of little faith?" "All things are possible to him that believeth."

Florence states that Fear is misdirected energy and must be redirected or transmuted into faith.

Fear in our physical world mind is very real and will eat us alive if we allow it to. It even has the ability to manifest itself into very frightening things through the power that we give it, yet it is still an illusion. However, we have the power to dissipate it from our lives. It is, indeed, a choice.

As Florence points out, when we walk up to the thing that we are most afraid of, it will dissolve into its native nothingness. Even though fear is real in our physical world minds, it is but a figment of man's imagination – an illusion. We create it – there is *no fear* in God.

We've learned that God does not need time and God is never late. We've also learned that God is our supply in all things. There is no need to think that God doesn't know how important a reliable car is for transportation – He does know. Or how important a roof over our head is – God gets this. The question is, ***do we* get how powerful God is?** Do we truly understand that Our Holy Father created the galaxies, flowers and the miracles of life? God knows how to put physical bodies together and make them work when He breathes life into them. Don't you think He can handle whatever issue it is that we're trying to deal with? Trusting God to take over the reigns of our lives is challenging and requires living from a source of love NOT fear in complete trust and faith.

It is through our complete Trust and Faith that God can dissipate that which we are fearful of. No matter what is going on around us, if we trust completely in God, we are not fearful. Even if we are facing death of our physical body, if we trust completely in God, there is no fear. Isn't this how we *really* want to live our lives?

Florence suggests monitoring our motives hourly to determine the basis for what we do. In monitoring ourselves we discern: are our actions fear based or love based? Remember there is no in between.

WORKBOOK ITEM FIVE:

Sit quietly and think about something that is troubling you – such as a relationship, something at work, your finances or your health. Write the situation or condition down under the Issue. Then evaluate – are your feelings and thoughts fear based or love based?

HINT: If it is bothering you, it is fear based.

Implement the Healing Circle of Love or Sedona Method of Release to transmute the fear to love and write about the love feelings in the love column. When you finish using the release method, the "issue" should no longer be an issue.

Do this for all things that are troubling you.

When you use the Healing Circle of Love method to progress through the list, more will be revealed to you to resolve and heal. Answers and peace will you yours.

Fear Base versus Love Base Form

Issue	Fear	Love

Use the Journal Page to write about what you discovered by evaluating and releasing the fear associated with these situations in your life. Are you beginning to feel limitless? Empowered? Do you feel deep within you that you are worthy to receive good things?

JOURNAL PAGE:

GOD IS THE GIVER AND THE RECEIVER

Let us open our minds to understand God being the giver and the receiver. Each one of us has a God Part within, therefore; when we give to others, we are giving to the God Part within them - God being the giver and God being the receiver.

When we give, in love, to others, we elevate our vibrational frequency and the Universe "matches" high vibrational frequencies of prosperity back to us. As our God Part gives to others; our God Part also receives the good back from the act of giving.

NOTE: When we give, we *will* receive something back. If we refuse to accept the gift that is given back to us, we violate spiritual law by intentionally blocking gifts from the universe. This stops our flow of abundance as well as the person giving to us.

Know that man cannot _out give_ God. You will find that in giving to others, you will receive abundance from the Universe – from God. Try to out give Him and you will experience an avalanche of abundance!

WORKBOOK ITEM SIX:

The following activity will share God's love with others, elevate your vibrational frequency (know the Universe will "match" back to you what you give out) and have long reaching loving affects on others. In implementing one, a few, or all of these suggestions, you will consciously set in motion good, love based works. You will "seed" good things for yourself and you will be sharing with others blessings you have received – giving from your heart. You will learn you **cannot out give God!**

"Whatsoever a man soweth that shall he also reap."

Suggestions:

1. Pay for the meal of the person behind you at a drive through window.

2. Pay the toll for the vehicle behind you on a toll road and/or give a sucker or other candy to the person taking the toll.

3. As you are leaving a restaurant, pay for the meal of the table next to you. In paying as you are leaving, you are able to remain anonymous.

4. When checking out at the grocery store or Wal-Mart, purchase a gift card and give it to someone in line or give it to the manager or clerk to forward to the next person in line – this way you remain anonymous.

5. Contact a local elementary school and donate new underwear, socks coats, etc for the children – or donate cash.

6. Contact a local school, homeless shelter, nursing home or hospital and sponsor a child or family for Christmas.

7. Leave money in a drink machine or phone booth for the next person who comes along.

8. Leave a roll of quarters and/or laundry detergent with a note that it is a gift for the person who discovers it at a Laundromat.

9. Help someone who needs help.

10. Volunteer

This is so much fun! Talk about a natural high – giving to others – especially anonymously! Use the Journal Page to write about your experience in lovingly giving to others – how you give, what happened and how you felt – then journal the amazing gifts/blessings you receive. Be consciously aware so you don't unintentionally block your receipt of a sweet gift from God – they *will* be coming!

JOURNAL PAGE:

THE FOUTH DIMENSIONAL WORLD

The Fourth Dimensional World requires a shift in consciousness – an elevation of our vibrational level – a deeper look within to achieve a clear understanding…

In the fourth dimensional world there is no death, there is no birth, for the spirit lives eternally – only the physical body dies. In the fourth dimensional world there is no disease, no poverty, no judgment, no pain, no sorrow, no lack, no resentment and no envy.

The fourth dimensional world consists of love – pure unconditional love. Love so pure that it is more than our physical world minds can comprehend - loved ones who have crossed over talk about this.

Barbara Mark of Angelspeake explained death of the physical body and the crossing over of the spirit to me in 2005. Barbara transitioned in July, 2006. After her transition she told me, *"I was right when I told you that death of the physical body is but a breath. But transitioning from the physical body into the arms of God is so much more! It is more wondrous, more beautiful, more loving than the human brain can fathom."* As I experienced Barbara's message, the love and awe enveloped me in the most delightful hug of love. There is <u>nothing</u> I can compare it to.

(In 2008 my deceased father, Big Jim and I coauthored *Waiting in the Other Room* to help dissipate the fear we humans have of death. You may learn more at SoulKisses.com, WaitingInTheOther-Room.com or Amazon.com)

In achieving an understanding of the fourth dimensional world we will have acquired the trust and faith in God to allow His will to be done in our lives. We will then be able to *allow* the abundance God has for us to reach us and to pass it forward, to share it with others.

RECAP

Our mission here in the physical world is to achieve the complete faith, trust and understanding of God – to reach the Fourth Dimensional Realm of consciousness – the world of Divine Mind.

To achieve that level of consciousness and maintain it, it is necessary to eradicate the physical world teachings and conditioning of doubt and fear from our subconscious and conscious minds. Florence explains the process and channeled the tools to help us "allow God's will to be done."

This chapter of Casting the Burden – Impressing the Subconscious moves us to a level of understanding that leaves awe in the human brain. To attain fully a level of consciousness to understanding the fourth dimensional world will take time, patience and a firmly built bridge line to God.

It is possible.

The tools provided through *The Game of Life* and workbook will aid in achieving that level of consciousness. Your entourage of angels, guides and teachers will help you to become immune to the physical world teachings of fear and doubt. Work with your angelic team to maintain a grounding of consciousness. Your life will be easier and the prosperous abundance you desire will be quicker to manifest.

Your spiritual growth is blooming ten fold. Allow it to be. Pray. Ask God to make your life easier. Ask Him to give you the clear eyes to see Him around you. Ask Him to give you clear hearing and knowing to understand His presence and His guidance. Graciously allow yourself to receive these things…

Use the Journal Pages to evaluate what you have learned in this section. Be sure to thank your guides, teachers and angels for being in attendance and helping you to clearly understand God's work.

May you be profoundly blessed in this moment and in every moment after…

JOURNAL PAGES:

JOURNAL PAGES continued:

Every man on this planet is taking his initiation in love. "A new commandment I give unto you, that ye love one another." Ouspensky states, in "Tertium Organum," that "love is a cosmic phenomenon," and opens to man the fourth dimensional world, "The World of the Wondrous."

Real love is selfless and free from fear. It pours itself out upon the object of its affection, without demanding any return. Its joy is in the joy of giving. Love is God in manifestation, and the strongest magnetic force in the universe. Pure, unselfish love *draws to itself its own*; it does not need to seek or demand. Scarcely anyone has the faintest conception of real love. Man is selfish, tyrannical or fearful in his affections, thereby losing the thing he loves. Jealousy is the worst enemy of love, for the imagination runs riot, seeing the loved one attracted to another, and invariably these fears objectify if they are not neutralized.

For example: A woman came to me in deep distress. The man she loved had left her for other women, and said he never intended to marry her. She was torn with jealousy and resentment and said she hoped he would suffer as he had made her suffer; and added, "How could he leave me when I loved him so much?"

I replied, "You are not loving that man, you are hating him," and added, "*You can never receive what you have never given. Give a perfect love and you will receive a perfect love.* Perfect yourself on this man. Give him a perfect, unselfish love, demanding nothing in return, do not criticize or condemn, and *bless him wherever his is.*"

She replied, "No, I won't bless him unless I know where he is!" she said.

"Well," I said, "that is not real love."

"When you *send out real love,* real love will return to you, either from this man or his equivalent, for if this man is not the divine selection, you will not want him. As you are one with God, you are one with the love which belongs to you by divine right."

Several months passed, and matters remained about the same, but she was working conscientiously with herself.

I said, "When you are no longer disturbed by his cruelty, he will cease to be cruel, as you are attracting it through your own emotions."

Then I told her of a brotherhood in India, who never said, "Good Morning" to each other. They used these words: *"I salute the Divinity in you."* They saluted the divinity in every man, and in the wild animals in the jungle, and they were never harmed, for they *saw only God in every* living thing. I said, "Salute the divinity in this man, and say, 'I see your divine self only. I see you as God sees you, perfect, made in His image and likeness.'"

She found she was becoming more poised, and gradually losing her resentment. He was a Captain, and she always called him "The Cap."

One day, she said, suddenly, *"God bless the Cap wherever he is."*

I replied: "Now that is real love, and when you have become a 'complete circle,' and are no longer disturbed by the situation, you will have his love, or attract its equivalent."

I was moving at this time, and did not have a telephone, so was out of touch with her for a few weeks, when one morning I received a letter saying, "We are married."

At the earliest opportunity, I paid her a call. My first words were, "What happened?"

"Oh," she exclaimed, "a miracle! One day I woke up and all suffering had ceased. I saw him that evening and he asked me to marry him. We were married in about a week, and I have never seen a more devoted man."

There is an old saying: *"No man is your enemy, no man is your friend, every man is your teacher."*

So one should become impersonal and learn what each man has to teach him, and soon he would learn his lessons and be free.

The woman's lover was teaching her selfless love, which every man, sooner or later, must learn.

Suffering is not necessary for man's development; it is the result of violation of spiritual law, but few people seem able to rouse themselves from their "soul sleep" without it. When people are happy, they usually become selfish, and automatically the law of Karma is set in action. Man often suffers loss through lack of appreciation.

I knew a woman who had a very nice husband, but she said often, "I don't care anything about being married, but that is nothing against my husband. I'm simply not interested in married life."

She had other interests, and scarcely remembered she had a husband. She only thought of him when she saw him. One day her husband told her he was in love with another woman, and left. She came to me in distress and resentment.

I replied, "It is exactly what you spoke the word for. You said you didn't care anything about being married, so the subconscious worked to get you unmarried."

She said, "Oh yes, I see. People get what they want, and then feel very much hurt."

She soon became in perfect harmony with the situation, and knew they were both much happier apart.

When a woman becomes indifferent or critical, and ceases to be an inspiration to her husband, he misses the stimulus of their early relationship and is restless and unhappy.

A man came to me dejected, miserable and poor. His wife was interested in the "Science of Numbers," and had had him read. It seems the report was not very favorable, for he said, "My wife says I'll never amount to anything because I am a two."

I replied, "I don't care what your number is, you are a perfect idea in divine mind, and we will demand the success and prosperity which are already planned for you by that Infinite Intelligence."

Within a few weeks, he had a very fine position, and a year or two later, he achieved a brilliant success as a writer. No man is a success in business unless he loves his work. The picture the artist paints for love (of his art) is his greatest work. The pot-boiler is always something to live down.

No man can attract money if he despises it. Many people are kept in poverty by saying: "Money means nothing to me, and I have a contempt for people who have it."

This is the reason so many artists are poor. Their contempt for money separates them from it.

I remember hearing one artist say of another, "He's no good as an artist, he has money in the bank."

This attitude of mind, of course, separates man from his supply; he must be in harmony with a thing in order to attract it.

Money is God in manifestation, as freedom from want and limitation, but it must be always kept in circulation and put to right uses. Hoarding and saving react with grim vengeance.

This does not mean that man should not have houses and lots, stocks and bonds, for "the barns of the righteous man shall be full." It means man should not hoard even the principal, if an occasion arises, when money is necessary. In letting it go out fearlessly and cheerfully he opens the way for more to come in, for God is man's unfailing and inexhaustible supply.

This is the spiritual attitude towards money and the great Bank of the Universal never fails!

We see an example of hoarding in the film production of "Greed." The woman won five thousand dollars in a lottery, but would not spend it. She hoarded and saved, let her husband suffer and starve, and eventually she scrubbed floors for a living.

She loved the money itself and put it above everything, and one night she was murdered and the money taken from her.

This is an example of where "love of money is the root of all evil." Money in itself, is good and beneficial, but used for destructive purposes, hoarded and saved, or considered more important than love, brings disease and disaster, and the loss of the money itself.

Follow the path of love, and all things are added, *for God is love, and God is supply*; follow the path of selfishness and greed, and the supply vanishes, or man is separated from it.

For example; I knew the case of a very rich woman, who hoarded her income. She rarely gave anything away, but bought and bought things for herself.

She was very fond of necklaces, and a friend once asked her how many she possessed. She replied, "Sixty-seven."

She bought them and put them away, carefully wrapped in tissue paper. Had she used the necklaces it would have been quite legitimate, but she was violating "the law of use." Her closets were filled with clothes she never wore, and jewels which never saw the light.

The woman's arms were gradually becoming paralyzed from holding on to things, and eventually she was considered incapable of looking after her affairs and her wealth was handed over to others to manage.

So man, in ignorance of the law, brings about his own destruction.

All disease, all unhappiness, come from the violation of the law of love. Man's boomerangs of hate, resentment and criticism, come back laden with sickness and sorrow. Love seems almost a lost art, but the man with the knowledge of spiritual law knows it must be regained, for without it, he has "become as sounding brass and tinkling cymbals."

For example: I had a student who came to me, month after month, to clean her consciousness of resentment.

After a while, she arrived at the point where she resented only one woman, but that one woman kept her busy.

Little by little she became poised and harmonious, and one day, all resentment was wiped out.

She came in radiant, and exclaimed "You can't understand how I feel! The woman said something to me and instead of being furious I was loving and kind, and she apologized and was perfectly lovely to me. No one can understand the marvelous lightness I feel within!"

Love and good-will are invaluable in business.

For example: A woman came to me, complaining of her employer. She said she was cold and critical and knew she did not want her in the position.

"Well," I replied, "Salute the Divinity in the woman and send her love."

She said "I can't; she's a marble woman."

I answered, "You remember the story of the sculptor who asked for a certain piece of marble. He was asked why he wanted it, and he replied, 'because there is an angel in the marble,' and out it he produced a wonderful work of art."

She said, "Very well, I'll try it." A week later she came back and said, "I did what you told me to, and now the woman is very kind, and took me out in her car."

People are sometimes filled with remorse for having done someone an unkindness, perhaps years ago.

If the wrong cannot be righted, its effect can be neutralized by doing some one a kindness *in the present.*

"This one thing I do, forgetting those things which are behind and reaching forth unto those things where are before."

Sorrow, regret and remorse tear down the cells of the body, and poison the atmosphere of the individual.

A woman said to me in deep sorrow, "Treat me to be happy and joyous, for my sorrow makes me so irritable with members of my family that I keep making more Karma."

I was asked to treat a woman who was mourning for her daughter. I denied all belief in loss and separation, and affirmed that God was the woman's joy, love and peace.

The woman gained her poise at once, but sent word by her son, not to treat any longer, because she was "so happy, it wasn't respectable."

So "mortal mind" loves to hang on to its griefs and regrets."

I knew a woman who went about bragging of her troubles, so, of course, she always had something to brag about.

The old idea was if a woman did not worry about her children, she was not a good mother.

Now, we know that mother-fear is responsible for many of the diseases and accidents which come into the lives of children.

For fear pictures vividly the disease or situation feared, and these pictures objectify, if not neutralized.

Happy is the mother who can say sincerely, that she puts her child in God's hands, and knows therefore, that he is divinely protected.

For example: A woman awoke suddenly, in the night, feeling her brother was in great danger. Instead of giving in to her fears, she commenced making statements of Truth, saying, "Man is a perfect idea in Divine Mind, and is always in his right place, therefore, my brother is in his right place, and is divinely protected."

The next day she found that her brother had been in close proximity to an explosion in a mine, but had miraculously escaped.

So man is his brother's keeper (in thought) and every man should know that the thing he loves dwells in "the secret place of the most high, and abides under the shadow of the Almighty."

"There shall no evil befall thee, neither shall any plague come nigh thy dwelling."

"Perfect love casteth out fear. He that feareth is not made perfect in love," and "Love is the fulfilling of the Law."

In this session:

- Unconditional Love and the Fourth Dimensional World
- One With God
- Suffering and Man's Development
- Success and Love
- Abundance Blocks
- Disease and Resentment
- Grief
- Mother – Fear and Worry
- Recap and Journal Pages

Begin this session by asking Archangel Michael to surround you with God's Divine White Light of Protection and set your intention to connect with your higher self – the God Part within.

Father, Mother, God, Creator of All That Is…

I claim my personal power and open the way to see clearly my field of potentiality, my field of infinite possibilities. I cut the ties of beliefs and thought patterns that no longer serve me in all directions of time thereby removing them from my consciousness, my subconscious and my superconscious. I fearlessly step into the magnificence of the true essence of who I am – One with God. I graciously accept all that is mine by divine right, under grace in a miraculous way and commit to fulfill all that I came to be, have and do in this incarnation on Mother Earth at this time.

Amen

Ask your guides, angels and teachers to be present with you to help you open your heart, mind and spirit to the infinite possibilities. Use your free will wisely and ask that *God's will* be done in your life.

Suffering is NOT necessary for man's development;
it is the result of violation of Spiritual Law.

UNCONDITIONAL LOVE AND THE FOURTH DIMENSIONAL WORLD

Florence states that "Love is God in manifestation, and the strongest magnetic force in the universe. Pure, unselfish love draws to itself its own; it does not need to seek or demand."

Our angels tell us our mission is to love. Man "loves" everything: oranges, the color blue, the Dallas Cowboys, a new car. We love the new partner in our lives. It takes great maturity to love unconditionally – to love unselfishly – to allow love to "be."

The *Game of Life* teaches us to look within – to eradicate the behaviors that are negative – to forgive ourselves and others – to connect with the God Part within and learn to love and honor ourselves. Until we do this, we really aren't capable of unconditional love, for we are conditioned by society to be fearful of true love – it's painful. Love is only painful when we put expectations and demands on it. Expecting and/or demanding specific behavior is a form of control – control stems from fear – fear makes us a magnet for what we are fearful of - writing our subconscious record with fear manifests disaster in concern to our love. The pattern becomes clear.

In the example Florence shared of the woman in love with the man "Cap" we see how in the beginning, the woman's "love" was possessive and controlling – fear was in charge. Through her trust in God to bring to her the love/man who was hers by divine right, she transmuted her fears. When she reached the stage of no longer being disturbed by the situation unconditional love was free to flow and her highest good of true love came to her.

Unconditional love has no hidden agenda, no demands, and no expectations.

Unconditional love allows the giver to receive in return the supreme joy of giving love.

God loves all unconditionally. No matter what we do, no matter who we are. As we allow our minds to take in all the basics of true, pure love we are elevated to a higher spiritual level – we understand more fully the concept of the Fourth Dimensional World and the profound depths of the words: trust, faith and love.

ONE WITH GOD

Man has the ability to be selfless in love. Man chooses to judge people instead of honoring the God Part within them. As we progress through *The Game of Life* and the workbook, we begin to understand the divinity within each one of us. We begin to see glimpses of the wholesome, pure love of God and the Fourth Dimensional World. As we become one with God, we discover that there are no physical words to describe the joy of being wrapped in the arms of God.

WORKBOOK ITEM ONE

This exercise is designed to waken your mind to the God Part within others. Your daily life on the planet earth involves the very real feelings of hatred and bigotry toward one other. If each human honored the God Part within the other, there would be no hatred, no bigotry, and no wars.

Let's face it, you have people in your life that irritate you – people who get under your skin and push your buttons. Sit quietly and think about the person – feel the discord in your chest? Write their name in the form and describe what it is about them that irritates and annoys you and the feelings that are rumbling within you.

NOTE: Irritation and annoyance are fear based emotions. People who irritate us are actually mirroring back to us things we do not like about ourselves. When we transmute the fear based feelings of irritation and annoyance to love using the Healing Circle of Love method we will not only heal the relationship with others but will heal the issues within us.

There are no paintings of God floating around, so instead, picture Jesus. Under His name, write the feelings glowing within you – the love.

Now picture the person giving you issues, then visualize Jesus face blending semi-transparently over the face of your person. Speak the words, "I salute the Divinity in you. I honor the God Part of you." Speak these words from deep within you – not just with your lips, but from your heart.

Write about the experience of transmuting your feelings in the appropriate column. Use the Healing Circle of Love to transmute completely your feelings to love.

Saluting the Divinity – Honoring the God Part Form

Your Person's Name: _____

Jesus:

Use the Journal Page to write about your experience in honoring the God Part within others. How did you feel the next time you thought of the person? How did you feel the next time you saw them? What did you learn about yourself?

Inharmony or discord with others is a transfer of our power to the other person. When we truly honor the God Part within others, we take our power back completely. The behavior of the person no longer affects us – no matter what they do, they cannot "get to us" or "push our buttons" – we are non-resistant. We are now free to move forward in our lives sharing the love of God with all we meet.

JOURNAL PAGE:

SUFFERING AND MAN'S DEVELOPMENT

Florence states "suffering is not necessary for man's development; it is the result of violation of spiritual law." The physical world teaches us that we must suffer to have abundance in our lives. We're taught through many organized religions that God is punishing and judgmental – feelings of unworthiness often times stem from this teaching.

Plus when we believe we must suffer during our life time in the physical world we write Suffering as a record in our subconscious. The subconscious then works diligently to manifest suffering in our lives. This record must be rewritten!

The reality is that God loves us unconditionally and has great, unlimited abundance for us – all we must do is allow ourselves to receive it. We don't have to look outside ourselves to find happiness. True happiness, love and contentment are within us. By looking within and working with our God Part, our superconscious, we will grow spiritually with wisdom. Our lives will change – some instantaneously. The teachings of Florence Scovel Shinn have created avalanches of growth and development. And you are choosing not to suffer, but to graciously accept God's bounty from a love based foundation of belief.

The reality is that we live in an abundance universe and we each have a magnificent, limitless Field of Potentiality. As stated before, the universe does not differentiate between our desire for a tissue or a drink of water or a new house or new car – it merely matches vibration to vibration.

WORKBOOK ITEM TWO

We are now in Chapter 7 of *The Game of Life*. In the past seven sessions your life has undergone a tremendous shift. Sit quietly and review the tools and Universal Laws you have learned and the changes you have implemented in your life. Now think back about your life before the book and workbook. Think about a limiting thought pattern, belief, attitude or habit that you practiced that brought you suffering. Write it in the Before/Suffering column. In the After/Joy column, write down the tools you used to identify the behavior, what you did to correct it and the after effects of the change.

As you identify your fear based suffering stage and compare it to your new love based joy state even more things you can change will be revealed to you. Ask your angels for assistance.

Spiritual Development – Suffering vs Joy

Before/Suffering	After/Joy

Use the Journal Page to write about your discoveries. Are you seeing that you are using your tools more easily now? Are you recognizing negative behavior more quickly and taking the appropriate steps to change it? Is there a part of your square of life that is easier to maintain positive thought patterns and behaviors? Are you using your journal and tools to delve deeper into the parts of your square of life that still have negative issues?

This journal section is a profoundly powerful tool. As you look back at your progress you will continue to see this. Be wise – use it – don't skip it – JOURNAL!

JOURNAL PAGES:

JOURNAL PAGES continued:

SUCCESS AND LOVE

Many of us choose our work without consulting what we "love" to do. We fail to look within to find the spark that ignites our flame of creativity. In the "perfect idea of divine mind," there is a fulfilling service for pay for each of us. It may not be what our families want us to do or our friend or even our logical, physical world mind. However, in divine mind, there is an important place for us to share our talents and gifts with the world. Finding this work is true success – the rewards are fulfilled love and a deep joy within at the ability to bring the service to the world.

Connecting with the God Part within and accepting the undying, unconditional support of God and our entourage of angels, teachers and guides give us strength to bring to fruition work that we love. Trusting completely in God as our supply lights the way to this work – we are in the right place at the right time, and/or we unknowingly have the skills to perform the work, and/or we have the opportunity to acquire further education that leads to the work. The guidance is provided when the trust is acquired.

WORKBOOK ITEM THREE

In previous chapters we've looked within to learn to recognize and get to know the God Part within. We've learned to connect with our guides, teachers and angels through automatic dictation and meditation. In this exercise we will revisit connecting to evaluate our life path.

Sit quietly and set the intent to connect/meditate with your God Part within. Look back at the past few weeks and feel the exhilaration of your spiritual growth – experience the gratitude of receipt of a more joy filled life. Ask you guides, teachers and/or angels more about your life path – about your square of life. Explore the possibilities of each area. Ask for clear guidance and clear signs. Use Sacred Space ~ Build It and They Will Come.

Use the Journal Page to write about your experience during your connection – you may want to use both the automatic dictation and meditation in order to be sure you are clear. How does the experience compare to previous experiences. Were you more confident? More comfortable? If you are confused or unsure of anything you learned, ask your guides and angels to clarify. Ask all the questions you have. Allow the answer to come to you. Write down all that comes to you and review.

JOURNAL PAGE:

ABUNDANCE BLOCKS

Man uses his thoughts, beliefs and words to block receipt of abundance. Florence shares with us the example of an artist whose contempt of money effectively blocked his attracting money to him. His contempt for money wrote in his subconscious record that money was bad so the artist received none.

Florence states that "Money is God in manifestation, as freedom from want and limitation, but it must be kept in circulation and put to right uses. Hoarding and saving react with grim vengeance."

Let's take a moment and get our minds around, "Money is God in manifestation, as freedom from want and limitation." This tells us that to become one with God does not mean that we will live our lives in lack and limitation and we won't want more. It means that money IS simply energy – a form of supply.

"Hoarding and saving react with grim vengeance" tells us that holding on to money with fear negates our belief that God is our supply, thereby blocking our continued receipt of cash. Circulation of our money with joy and gratitude shows active faith that God is our unlimited supply.

We are reminded that good things coming to us are not rewards for good behavior. They are our birthright – including receiving money. With God as our supply, there is no room for fear of lack – of not having enough money. We are to give our money fearlessly – for then we are in control of it. Money is not in control of us.

"In letting it go out fearlessly and cheerfully" man "opens the way for more to come in, for God is man's unfailing and inexhaustible supply. This is the spiritual attitude towards money and the great Bank of the Universal never fails!"

Florence shows us clearly the "love of money is the root of all evil" through the example of the woman who hoarded money and was eventually murdered for it. "Money in itself is good and beneficial" for it is "God in manifestation, as freedom from want and limitation."

We learned in Chapter Six that we cannot out give God. The more we give in love, the more the Universe works to "match" to us freely, lovingly giving. It is the Universal Law of Attraction.

WORKBOOK ITEM FOUR

Look within and discern your thoughts, feelings and beliefs about money. Are you afraid to let it go? Do you pay bills with gratitude as if you have a limitless supply – more than you can spend? Or do you pay bills riddled with fear? If you are experiencing fear, use the Healing Circle of Love method to transmute your fear where money is concerned to love.

Use the Journal Page to write about your experience in transmuting your fear to love. Did your entire world shift? Do you feel lighter than air? Do you feel free and limitless?

JOURNAL PAGE:

DISEASE AND RESENTMENT

"All disease, all unhappiness, come from the violation of the law of love. Man's boomerangs of hate, resentment and criticism, come back laden with sickness and sorrow." Throughout *The Game of Life* and the workbook we've experienced changes in each section of our square of life as we have become more spiritually evolved. Through our workbook exercises and journaling we've learned to identify negativity and through our tools we now know how to be rid of it. We are coming to understand the importance of living from a foundation of love.

At each juncture of changing our thought patterns and beliefs, we've learned new things about ourselves. We are learning how to become immune to the negativity of the physical world and focus on the true, pure love of God and light within. We are consciously making a choice to work with God instead of constantly fighting for control of things we have no control over. We are vastly improving our quality of life.

GRIEF

"Sorrow, regret and remorse tear down the cells of the body, and poison the atmosphere of the individual." Physical world conditioning teaches us to live in guilt and regret – this is living in the past – not in the moment. The physical world also teaches us that death is bad. When we are truly connected with our God Part within, we know that God is our "joy, love and peace." Physical world conditioning is all about the physical world – there is no God – there is fear.

Grief is a physical world emotion that we must experience because our spirits are living in a human body. It is *very* important that we allow ourselves to experience grief for the loss of loved ones who transition, for the loss of a job, for moving, for children moving out. Anything that causes our physical world presence pain, we must grieve for. However, it is a violation of spiritual law to wallow in it. We must hold fast to our trust and faith in God as our supply. As we come to a better understanding and connection with the Fourth Dimensional World, this will become easier to do. The challenges of the physical world will become easier.

The Sedona Method® of Release and the Healing Circle of Love are a remarkable tools to help deal with grief of any kind.

WORKBOOK ITEM FIVE

Grief is an emotion we have not addressed. Evaluate your life. Do you have any lingering feelings of grief? Use The Sedona Method® of release to help you to resolve feelings of grief.

Use the Healing Circle of Love to transmute lingering feelings of grief to love. Use the Journal Page to write about your experience in dissipating grief.

JOURNAL PAGE:

MOTHER – FEAR AND WORRY

"Now, we know that mother-fear is responsible for many of the diseases and accidents which come into the lives of children."

We've learned how fear blocks the love of God from helping us – from bringing abundance to us. It also blocks receipt of healing. Fearing for ourselves, our children, our loved ones, effectively blocks receipt of help from God. Fear is in charge and in control of our lives.

Fear does nothing to enhance our lives.

We are learning to consciously make the choice to live in a foundation of love – not fear/negativity. If we are truly love based, we are protected from the affects of fear based thoughts.

Transmuting fear and worry to a love base doesn't mean we don't care. On the contrary, it proves our faith and trust in God. It is easier to worry. We're conditioned by the physical world to be fearful and to worry. It is proof of our love to make the effort to transmute fear and worry to love – making ourselves and our loved one a magnet for more love. When we release fear where another individual is concerned we open the way for us and them to step more fully into personal power.

WORKBOOK ITEM SIX

Sit quietly and think of those you love. Do you feel any worry, anxiousness, frustration, guilt or fear where they are concerned? Use the Healing Circle of Love method to transmute your fear to love.

Use the Journal Page to write about your love experience. Do you feel peace and an inner joy when you think about your loved one?

JOURNAL PAGE:

RECAP

When the angels are asked what our life mission is, they tell us, Love. What exactly does this mean? This chapter of Love details bringing love into the physical world. Achieving a state of unconditional love will change the life of the individual. Collectively achieving a state of unconditional love will change the world.

We're grasping a better concept of the Fourth Dimensional Realm and seeing a better glimpse of it. Our goal of becoming One with God is becoming more a part of our every day life instead of something we only wonder about.

We've learned more about our divine life path and are feeling the divine guidance to walk it. The abundance blocks that were ingrained in us before are becoming easier to recognize and dismantle.

Maintaining a positive focus and deflecting negativity has become much easier.

Your level of spiritual enlightenment has blossomed as the days have passed. Do not become discouraged if parts of the workbook are confusing. Simply move on and when you have time, go back to anything you didn't quite grasp. As you move through the book and workbook, items that were once confusing will become clearer.

Continue to journal – daily if you possibly can. Your journal is a direct gateway to connecting with God and maintaining balance of your three levels of consciousness. It always will be. Daily journaling will bring forward more and more information, more understanding, and more spiritual growth.

When you have a moment, go back through the workbook and identify any areas that may be weak. Review your journal for insights as to why. Use the tools you have learned to transmute the weakness.

Be sure to thank your guides, teachers and angels for being in attendance and helping you to clearly understand God's work.

May you be profoundly blessed in this moment and in every moment after…

JOURNAL PAGES:

JOURNAL PAGES continued:

Chapter 8 - Intuition and Guidance

"In all thy ways acknowledge Him and He shall direct thy paths."

There is nothing too great of accomplishment for the man who knows the power of his word, and who follows his intuitive leads. By the word he starts in action unseen forces and can rebuild his body or remold his affairs.

It is, therefore, of the utmost importance, to choose the right words, and the student carefully selects the affirmation he wishes to catapult into the invisible.

He knows that God is his supply, that there is a supply for every demand, and that his spoken word releases this supply.

"Ask and ye shall receive."

Man must make the first move. "Draw nigh to God and He will draw nigh to you."

I have often been asked just how to make a demonstration.

I reply: "Speak the word and then do not do anything until you get a definite lead." Demand the lead, saying, "Infinite spirit, reveal to me the way, let me know if there is anything for me to do."

The answer will come through intuition (or hunch); a chance remark from someone, or a passage in a book, etc., etc. The answers are sometimes quite startling in their exactness. For example: A woman desired a large sum of money. She spoke the words: "Infinite Spirit, open the way for my immediate supply, let all that is mine by divine right now reach me, in great avalanches of abundance." Then she added: "Give me a definite lead, let me know if there is anything for me to do."

The thought came quickly, "Give a certain friend" (who had helped her spiritually) "a hundred dollars." She told her friend, who said, "Wait and get another lead, before giving it." So she waited, and that day met a woman who said to her, "I gave someone a dollar today; it was just as much for me, as it would be for you to give someone a hundred."

This was indeed an unmistakable lead, so she knew she was right in giving the hundred dollars. It was a gift which proved a great investment, for shortly after that, a large sum of money came to her in a remarkable way.

Giving opens the way for receiving. In order to create activity in finances, one should give. Tithing or giving one-tenth of one's income, is an old Jewish custom, and is sure to bring increase. Many of the richest men in this country have been tithers, and I have never known it to fail as an investment.

The tenth-part goes forth and returns blessed and multiplied. But the gift or tithe must be given with love and cheerfulness, for "God loveth a cheerful giver." Bills should be paid cheerfully, all money should be sent forth fearlessly and with a blessing.

This attitude of mind makes man master of money. It is his to obey, and his spoken word then opens vast reservoirs of wealth.

Man, himself, limits his supply by his limited vision. Sometimes the student has a great realization of wealth, but is afraid to act.

The vision and action must go hand in hand, as in the case of the man who bought the fur-lined overcoat.

A woman came to me asking me to "speak the word" for a position. So I demanded: "Infinite Spirit, open the way for this woman's right position." Never ask for just "a position"; ask for the right position, the place already planned in Divine Mind, as it is the only one that will give satisfaction.

I then gave thanks that she had already received, and that it would manifest quickly. Very soon, she had three positions offered her, two in New York and one in Palm Beach, and she did not know which to choose. I said,

"Ask for a definite lead."

The time was almost up and was still undecided, when one day, she telephoned, "When I woke up this morning, I could smell Palm Beach." She had been there before and knew its balmy fragrance.

I replied: "Well, if you can smell Palm Beach from here, it is certainly your lead." She accepted the position, and it proved a great success. Often one's lead comes at an unexpected time.

One day, I was walking down the street, when I suddenly felt a strong urge to go to a certain bakery, a block or two away.

The reasoning mind resisted, arguing, "There is nothing there that you want."

However, I had learned not to reason, so I went to the bakery, looked at everything, and there was certainly nothing there that I wanted, but coming out I encountered a woman I had thought of often, and who was in great need of the help which I could give her.

So often, one goes for one thing and finds another.

Intuition is a spiritual faculty and does not explain, but simply *points the way*.

A person often receives a lead during a "treatment." The idea that comes may seem quite irrelevant, but some of God's leadings are "mysterious."

In the class, one day, I was treating that each individual would receive a definite lead. A woman came to me afterwards, and said: "While you were treating, I got the hunch to take my furniture out of storage and get an apartment." The woman had come to be treated for health. I told her I knew in getting a home of her own, her health would improve, and I added, "I believe your trouble, which is a congestion, has come from having things stored away. Congestion of things causes congestion in the body. You have violated the law of use, and your body is paying the penalty."

So I gave thanks that "*Divine order was established in her mind, body and affairs.*"

People little dream of how their affairs react on the body. There is a mental correspondence for every disease. A person might receive instantaneous healing through the realization of his body being a perfect idea in Divine Mind, and, therefore, whole and perfect, but if he continues his destructive thinking, hoarding, hating, fearing, condemning, the disease will return.

Jesus Christ knew that all sickness came from sin, but admonished the leper after the healing, to go and sin no more, lest a worse thing come upon him.

So man's soul (or subconscious mind) must be washed whiter than snow, for permanent healing; and the metaphysician is always delving deep for the "correspondence."

Jesus Christ said, "Condemn not lest ye also be condemned."

"Judge not, lest ye be judged."

Many people have attracted disease and unhappiness through condemnation of others.

What man condemns in others, he attracts to himself.

For example: A friend came to me in anger and distress, because her husband had deserted her for another woman. She condemned the other woman, and said continually, "She knew he was a married man, and had no right to accept his attentions."

I replied: "Stop condemning the woman, bless her, and be through with the situation, otherwise, you are attracting the same thing to yourself."

She was deaf to my words, and a year or two later, became deeply interested in a married man, herself.

Man picks up a live-wire whenever he criticizes or condemns, and may expect a shock.

Indecision is a stumbling-block in many a pathway. In order to overcome it, make the statement repeatedly, "*I am always under direct inspiration; I make right decisions, quickly.*"

These words impress the subconscious, and soon one finds himself awake and alert, making his right moves without hesitation. I have found it destructive to look to the psychic plane for guidance, as it is the plane of many minds and not the "The One Mind."

As man opens his mind to subjectivity, he becomes a target for destructive forces. The psychic plane is the result of man's mortal thought, and is on the "plane of opposites." He may receive either good or bad messages.

The science of numbers and the reading of horoscopes, keep man down on the mental (or mortal) plane, for they deal only with the Karmic path.

I know of a man who should have been dead, years ago, according to his horoscope, but he is alive and a leader of one of the biggest movements in this country for the uplift of humanity.

It takes a very strong mind to neutralize a prophecy of evil. The student should declare, "Every false prophecy shall come to naught; every plan my Father in heaven has not planned, shall be dissolved and dissipated, the divine idea now comes to pass."

However, if any good message has ever been given one, of coming happiness, or wealth, harbor and expect it, and it will manifest sooner or later, through the law of expectancy.

Man's will should be used to back the universal will. "I will that the will of God be done."

It is God's will to give every man, every righteous desire of his heart, and man's will should be used to hold the perfect vision, without wavering.

The prodigal son said: "I will arise and go to my Father."

It is indeed, often an effort of the will to leave the husks and swine of mortal thinking. It is so much easier, for the average person, to have fear than faith; *so faith is an effort of the will.*

As man becomes spiritually awakened he recognizes that any external inharmony is the correspondence of mental inharmony. If he stumbles or falls, he may know he is stumbling or falling in consciousness.

One day, a student was walking along the street condemning someone in her thoughts. She was saying mentally, "That woman is the most disagreeable woman on earth," when suddenly three boy scouts rushed around the corner and almost knocked her over. She did not condemn the boy scouts, but immediately called on the law of forgiveness, and "saluted the divinity" in the woman. Wisdom's way are ways of pleasantness and all her paths are peace.

When one has made his demands upon the Universal, he must be ready for surprises. Everything may seem to be going wrong, when in reality, it is going right.

For example: A woman was told that there was no loss in divine mind, therefore, she could not lose anything which belonged to her; anything lost, would be returned, or she would receive its equivalent.

Several years previously, she had lost two thousand dollars. She had loaned the money to a relative during her lifetime, but the relative had died, leaving no mention of it in her will. The woman was resentful and angry, and as she had no written statement of the transaction, she never received the money, so she determined to deny the loss, and collect the two thousand dollars from the Bank of the Universal. She had to begin by forgiving the woman, as resentment and unforgiveness close the doors of this wonderful bank.

She made this statement, "I deny loss, there is no loss in Divine Mind, therefore, I cannot lose the two thousand dollars, which belong to me by divine right. "*As one door shuts another door opens*."

She was living in an apartment house which was for sale; and in the lease was a clause, stating that if the house was sold, the tenants would be required to move out within ninety days.

Suddenly, the landlord broke the leases and raised the rent. Again, injustice was on her pathway, but this time she was undisturbed. She blessed the landlord, and said, "As the rent has been raised, it means that I'll be that much richer, for God is my supply."

New leases were made out for the advanced rent, but by some divine mistake, the ninety days clause had been forgotten. Soon after, the landlord had an opportunity to sell the house. On account of the mistake in the new leases, the tenants held possession for another year.

The agent offered each tenant two hundred dollars if he would vacate. Several families moved; three remained, including the woman. A month or two passed, and the agent again appeared. This time he said to the woman,

"Will you break your lease for the sum of fifteen hundred dollars?" It flashed upon her, "Here comes the two thousand dollars." She remembered having said to friends in the house, "We will all act together if anything more is said about leaving." So her lead was to consult her friends.

These friends said," Well, if they have offered you fifteen hundred they will certainly give two thousand." So she received a check for two thousand dollars for giving up the apartment. It was certainly a remarkable working of the law, and the apparent injustice was merely opening the way for her demonstration.

It proved that there is no loss, and when man takes his spiritual stand, he collects all that is his from this great Reservoir of Good.

"I will restore to you the years the locusts have eaten."

These adverse thoughts, alone, rob man; for "No man gives to himself but himself, and no man takes away from himself, but himself."

Man is here to prove God and "to bear witness to the truth," and he can only prove God by bringing plenty out of lack, and justice out of injustice.

"Prove me now herewith, saith the Lord of hosts, if I will not open you the windows of heaven, and pour out a blessing, that there shall not be room enough to receive it."

In this session:

- Intention/Claiming/Demand/Action is Everything
- Tithing/Giving Opens the Way for Receiving
- Action: Asking and Guidance/Intuition
- Congestion/Illness/Judgment & The Law of Attraction
- Psychic Discernment
- Open the Doors of Abundance
- External Inharmony
- No Loss in Divine Mind
- Man: the Giver and the Taker
- Recap and Journal Page

Begin this session by asking Archangel Michael to surround you with God's Divine White Light of Protection and set your intention to connect with your higher self – the God part within.

Father, Mother, God, Creator of All That Is…

I claim my personal power and open the way to see clearly my field of potentiality, my field of infinite possibilities. I cut the ties of beliefs and thought patterns that no longer serve me in all directions of time thereby removing them from my consciousness, my subconscious and my superconscious. I fearlessly step into the magnificence of the true essence of who I am – One with God. I graciously accept all that is mine by divine right, under grace in a miraculous way and commit to fulfill all that I came to be, have and do in this incarnation on Mother Earth at this time.

Amen

Ask your guides, angels and teachers to be present with you to help you open your heart, mind and spirit to the infinite possibilities.

Demand and Ye Shall Receive.

INTENTION/CLAIMING/DEMAND/ACTION IS EVERYTHING

Most of us put more thought into what we're going to do when we get off early than we do in creating the life we truly desire – sad but true. Or we focus our energies on "worry." What does worry do to enhance our lives? It does *nothing* to enhance it, but it *will* make us sick and it *will* make us a magnet for what we do *not* want.

We've learned that what we continually focus our energies on – our thought patterns and beliefs – will manifest in our lives – whether we do it consciously or unconsciously – this is the Universal Law of Attraction.

Florence tells us that by *"man's word he starts in action unseen forces and can rebuild his body or remold his affairs."*

In these words she tells us that we have the power to heal (rebuild) our bodies and change/improve (remold) our lives. The reality is that we do this every day. Whether it is consciously or unconsciously we choose daily what we focus on – and ultimately what we bring into our lives.

In accepting the **fact** that there is a Universal Supply and there *is enough* for everyone we set a foundation for bringing to fruition our desires through the vibrational frequency of our core base thoughts.

The Bible tells us, "Ask and ye shall receive." Florence uses the word "demand."

The dictionary states: to Ask is: "to make a request for; to expect or demand." In looking closer we see that the state of "asking" is based from a place of lack – a place of want – asking is a fear based thought. The dictionary's definition states asking is making a request for – clearly we don't have it or we wouldn't be asking for it – we're in a state of lack. However, the dictionary also states that to Ask is to expect or demand, lets look closer at this word/action: demand.

Demanding of God doesn't quite sound right – it sounds harsh, abrasive and perhaps a little arrogant, but when we go to the dictionary, it states Demand is: "to claim formally." "To claim formally" doesn't have such a critical connotation; instead the reality is that demanding what we desire is actually a love based action.

Remember every thought, every word and every action is either love based or fear based, therefore the subconscious human mind and the universe recognizes asking and demanding in this way:

To Ask **is a fear based thought pattern and action because it comes from a place of not having what we are asking to receive – lack, without.**

To Demand **is a love based thought pattern and action because it comes from a place of love –** **of having already received – claiming formally what is ours. It also shows active faith and trust in** **God as our supply – in effect, a compliment to God.**

The key here is to move ourselves from a place of lack and fear to a place of love and prosperous abundance. If at this point in your spiritual journey it isn't "in you" to "demand" of God, use the word "command."

When we discern what we truly desire and claim it as ours to the Universe/God (demand as Florence states) the act puts into action our desire – we set the intent.

To break it down:

1. Discern what we truly desire.

2. "Set the intent" by "claiming our desire formally as ours" – demand or command of the Universal Supply Warehouse/God

Through discernment we set into motion the "unseen forces that can rebuild (man's) body or remold his affairs." By claiming our desire as ours – we've eradicated fear based thought patterns and beliefs – we've claimed it, thereby, executing a state of receipt. It puts into our mind a belief that the object of our desire is already ours.

By claiming something that is already ours, it also eliminates the "how are we going to receive?" aspect or phase. In living the human experience, our predisposition is to try to figure out how we're going to receive what we want. This action stems from doubt, anxiety, lack and yes, fear. Trying to figure out "how" negates receipt of our desire because it is a fear based thought pattern. Releasing control to the universe and allowing guidance and direction through our intuition as to what action to take is the key.

Note: Know that our thought processes are heavily conditioned by the physical world. As a result our brain typically will begin to think "I'll never be able to do this, or have this, or receive this," thereby negating our claim for what we desire as well. Receiving abundance is our birthright – we are the children of God of All That Is. It is up to us as to whether we allow this negative, fear based thinking to be our focus or not.

The action of claiming our desire, anchors in our thought patterns the belief that what we desire is already ours. As a result of maintaining a love based in gratitude perspective, there are no worries, no doubts, and no anxieties of "how are we going to receive?"

The object of our desire is already ours in Divine Mind – now it is already ours in *our mind*.

Example: use of valet for our car or coat check for our coat. When we take the action of claiming our car or our coat, we experience the feeling of receiving that which is ours – our car or our coat. In claiming something we have discerned that we desire in our lives, we set the intent and initiate that feeling of receiving something that is already ours.

We've learned that we each have a limitless Field of Potentiality. In our Field of Potential are all that we dream and desire – it is already ours. So all we need do is claim what is ours by Divine Right – like we would claim our car from the valet.

We've discerned what we desire and we've claimed it as ours. Now is the time to ask/command/demand "a lead" as Florence terms it. Look within and ask the question what can I do to bring this desire to fruition?

The first step, of course is to be in gratitude of receipt as we claim our desire, but there may be a physical action to take. If we desire better health, we may be guided to research nutrition and exercise programs that fit our needs. If it is a relationship, we may be guided to focus on the positive things in the relationship and forgive the things that are negative. If it is a job, we may be guided to research classifieds, internet or put out feelers. If it is financial, we may be guided to look into how to invest large sums of money – even when we don't have two nickels to rub together. These actions continue to anchor in the universe receipt of our desire.

While taking the actions we are guided to take, it is important to maintain the attitude of gratitude of receipt. Completing our actions with an attitude of gratitude completely frees the universe to provide our desire to us in its miraculous way in its miraculous time.

Summary:
1. Discern Desire
2. Set Intent/Claim/Demand (command) Desire
3. Attitude of Gratitude
4. Action/Maintain Attitude of Gratitude

WORKBOOK ITEM ONE

You've learned how to discern what you truly desire, how to set the intention of receiving by claiming formerly or demanding your desire, the attitude of gratitude and how to implement action of receipt.

This exercise is designed to employ these things in a practical form.

1. Sit quietly and think about a small, insignificant item that you would like to receive or an experience that you would like to have. Discern what it is. Example: a feather, a specific coin, a heart shaped object. Write it in the space:

2. Set the intention of receiving the desire by claiming it formerly from God/the Universal Supply Warehouse. See the Universal Supply Warehouse form directly after this exercise. Write what it is like to fill out this form in the space:

3. Imagine how good it feels to enjoy the desire. Visualize - Make Believe - Experience Receipt! Now focus on the gratitude. Write in the space the visualization of the experience of receipt and the feeling of gratitude.

4. Ask/command/demand God/the Universe if there is anything you can do to bring your desire into your reality. Write down your guidance if there is any.

5. As you go about the routine of your day, think about your desire and maintain your attitude of gratitude of receipt. The universe *will* match your vibrational frequency in it's time. Write here about your results.

NOTE: Do NOT ask for money – ask for the item you would purchase with the money. Is there anything else you would like to anchor about this experience? Use the Journal Page space:

JOURNAL PAGE:

Universal Supply Warehouse Form:

Ask/Discern what you desire then fill in the form. Believe/Let it Happen/Attitude of Gratitude then allow yourself to receive with gratitude.

UNIVERSAL SUPPLY WAREHOUSE FORM

Description of What You Desire	Price
	By Divine Right
Shipping & Handling: Under Grace in a Wonderful Way	

Receipt Action: Be open to guidance of action to take (if any) to receive desire.

Delivery Details: As designed by God under grace by divine right in a perfect way.

Use the Journal Page to write about your experience. Did you negate your receipt of your desire with doubt and/or fear? Or did you maintain your attitude of gratitude and bring into your reality the object of your desire?

JOURNAL PAGE:

TITHING/GIVING OPENS THE WAY FOR RECEIVING

Florence states "giving opens the way for receiving. In order to create activity in finances, one should give." In times of financial distress the idea of "giving away money" is enough to send the physical part of us into a panic attack.

The reality is that giving money away without fear, as if you have more than you'll ever need, sends out a signal to the universe that you have all the money you'll ever need and the universe matches that frequency of vibration by "matching" to you more money.

This is how the Universal Law of Attraction works. Always.

Important Note: If money is given away in fear the action is fear based and will attract more fear. The emotion of fear is easy to identify within oneself when it comes to money. Identify your source of emotion before giving money away! Make sure it is love based!!

Giving cheerfully with love to others opens the door to receipt of same – joy, love, abundance and prosperity in what you freely, cheerfully, lovingly share. In giving with these emotions, your vibrational frequency is raised – the universe in turn matches to you that vibrational frequency of people, health, love and perfect self expression – the square of life.

Tithing is typically thought of as ten percent of one's income. Tithing may be given in many ways. A few examples are: cash, time and/or volunteering.

The key is looking within yourself to discern the best way for you to tithe to maintain the feeling of love, cheerfulness and gratitude. It may be giving cash to the beggar on the corner, or a check to the church, or donating a weekend of time every month to an assisted living facility or local hospital. Tithing can be creative and a LOT of fun!

Florence tells us that bills should be paid cheerfully. Typically the physical world conditioning of money makes paying bills a painful experience. Transmute this pain to gratitude by being thankful for the wonderful roof overhead provided by the mortgage or rent if your residence is less than you desire, demand a new one! Transmute the pain of the utility bill by being thankful for the warmth in winter and the cool in summer. Transmute the pain to gratitude and joy. It can be done – it is all in how we perceive the process.

REMEMBER: As we learned in Chapter 6, we cannot out give God!

WORKBOOK ITEM TWO

This exercise is designed to stir your creativity in tithing. Tithing is an important part of creating cash flow, yet it can be the cause of great anxiety. If tithing creates anxiety, it isn't based in love and you should not do it. The key is to base tithing in love and be a cheerful giver.

In the space provided, list out five ways you can tithe that will bring you great joy.

1.

2.

3.

4.

5.

Use the Journal Page to write about these ways of tithing. Then implement at least one way of tithing from the list this week. Implement all five if you can. As you practice the act of tithing, you'll discover which way brings you the most joy. Be sure to thank God/The Universe for things that you receive unexpectedly. Also, make a point to be a cheerful, gracious receiver! It is imperative that you allow yourself to receive graciously what the Universe/God sends to you – do NOT block the Universal flow of supply by refusing to receive!

JOURNAL PAGE:

ACTION: ASKING AND GUIDANCE/INTUITION

In claiming our desire as ours, as if we have already received, we've learned that we've eliminated the worries of "how will we receive?" Now providing what we desire is in the capable hands of God/The Universal Supply Warehouse.

We've looked within and we've asked, "What can I do to bring my desire to fruition?" And we get nothing. Some times there is nothing for us to do. Some times our job is just to go about our lives handling our responsibilities while maintaining an attitude of gratitude of having received what we desire.

Or we may get an inner nudge to go somewhere, or call someone, or to turn on the TV, or to purchase luggage for the trip we desire, or to pick up a book and read it. Our inner knowing, the God Part within, will point the way with this nudge. Follow it – explore where it takes you.

Following these leads or intuition will guide us, usually in a miraculous way, to receipt of what we desire. In truth it is our working with God/The Universe to bring to fruition our desire. All three levels of consciousness are working in tandem together.

WORKBOOK ITEM THREE

Sit in a quiet place and set the intention to look within – to connect with your God Part using the Sacred Space ~ Build It and They Will Come meditation. Focus on your breathing and open a dialogue with God about your life situations as they are now. Discuss what is in your highest good and ask for guidance on discerning what is best for you and the next step to take in bringing your desires to fruition.

Use the Journal Page to write about this experience, the questions you had and the answers you came to while connecting with God/the Universe.

JOURNAL PAGE:

CONGESTION-ILLNESS-JUDGMENT AND THE LAW OF ATTRACTION

Florence states that "congestion of things causes congestion in the body."

The physical world conditions us to live from a place of lack like we'll never have enough, therefore, we tend to hoard things – material things as well as our love for others. We hold on to it tightly like we will lose it if we relax – this is a fear based action. We've learned that fear based actions don't have good outcomes – they produce more fear and lack.

Fear will create illness in the body. The body does not function well on a diet of hoarding, hatred, fear, condemnation, judgment and unforgiveness.

James Arthur Ray, author, said, *"Being unforgiving is like swallowing poison and expecting the other person to die."* These feelings, emotions and thought patterns lower the vibrational frequency of the body and allow it to be a strong magnet for disease and illness.

Florence states: *"A person might receive instantaneous healing through the realization of his body being a perfect idea in Divine Mind, and, therefore, whole and perfect."* There is no room for fear in the perfect idea in Divine Mind – only love.

The Law of Attraction works whether we are consciously or unconsciously making the choice of what we want to attract in our lives. What we continually think about and practice in our lives is what we will attract to us. No one is immune to it – whether we know about it, understand it or work with it, the law affects all of us.

The physical world teaches us to judge everything. God does not judge us, but we continue to practice the judgment of others. Judgment is a fear based emotion and thought pattern – it is not love based. Forgiveness is a love based emotion and thought pattern.

WORKBOOK ITEM FOUR

This exercise is designed to evaluate where you are today in your ability to be non-resistant and allow others to be who they are. Look within and answer each question honestly.

1. Is there anyone in my life that I am angry with?

2. Is there anyone in my life that I continually judge?

3. Am I critical and judgmental of me?

4. When I look back at my life, do I find people and/or situations that still cause me pain and anxiety?

Use the Journal Page to write about these findings. Use The Sedona Method® of Release or the Healing Circle of Love to help you rid yourself of the fear/negative based thought patterns and beliefs.

JOURNAL PAGE:

PSYCHIC DISCERNMENT

In our human experience we are easily led. On average, people take what they are told to be truth. To compare church doctrines side by side we see that clearly they are different. Yet, typically, we take what our particular religion teaches without questioning it as to its accuracy. We accept what our teachers teach us without questioning the teachings.

The physical world conditions us to live in fear through a lot of these teachings. It is up to us as spiritual individuals to look within and to discern what the "truth" is.

We've learned how to look within, how to work with our God Part, our intuition to move forward to our highest good. God and our entourage of angels, teachers, guides and deceased loved ones want us to remember how to communicate with them directly.

There are among us those who have developed this line of communication and can do it for us – psychics and mediums. However it is still up to us to discern if these people are "of God and working in integrity." Unfortunately, not everyone works from God's love base with integrity. Look within to discern this before giving anyone permission to enter your space and communicate with your entourage.

Also, look honestly at your reasons for consulting a psychic or medium. Is it to have them tell you what to do? Or is it to validate what you are feeling within?

You are no longer a follower of physical world conditioning. You are a powerful, perceptive, insightful child of God. Use your tools of discernment to reach your highest good.

OPEN THE DOORS OF ABUNDANCE

Daily we are subjected to negativity, hatred, unforgiveness and fear – daily. This happens by radio, TV, road rage/traffic, coworkers, family members, etc. It is up to us to transmute the negativity to love.

We've learned that all our thoughts, emotions and feelings are either based in love or based in fear – there is no in between.

We've also learned that what we continually focus on we will attract to us. We are creating our future in every moment of our life. What we continually focus on WILL manifest into our lives as our reality.

We can look back at our lives and see how our negative feelings and thought patterns drew to us still more lack, fear, painful relationships and situations, illness, horrible employers or coworkers or friends or even family.

We have successfully created the current life we are living. The question is, "Is this the life we truly desire?"

The abundance of our square of life: health, wealth, love and perfect self-expression is directly related to our ability to live from a source of love. Fear based thought patterns and beliefs are not the key and will not open the door. Love based thought patterns and beliefs ARE the key!

Universal laws are continually at work in our lives whether we want to acknowledge it or not. Fussing about how things turned out is not going to change anything. Conditions that need to be changed are not changed by complaining about them – this would fuel yet more negativity. Conditions are changed with love. Negative, fear based thought patterns and beliefs create negative, fearful conditions. The conditions can be changed by transmuting the negative, fear based thought patterns and beliefs to love based thought patterns and beliefs.

When we change within, our reality change - miraculously doors to the abundance we desire open.

WORKBOOK ITEM FIVE

This exercise is designed to discover what your focus was today. Please read each question and answer it honestly.

1. What were my feelings when I woke this morning? Happy? Sad? Anxious?

2. As I moved through the first half of my day, how did I allow the physical world to affect me if at all? (Examples: I tripped over toys and became irritated or I tripped over toys and remembered how grateful I am for the joy of watching child/dog play with toys. Traffic was a mess and I was worried about being late or traffic was a mess and I used the time to breathe deeply and center myself)

3. Evaluate the experience of the second half of the day. Was it a loving positive experience or was it fear based, producing anxiety?

4. Was there a point during the day that I recognized fear based negative thoughts coming into my mind and I transmuted them to love?

5. Did I live consciously today or unconsciously?

Use the Journal Page to write about your discoveries. Did you catch yourself experiencing fear based moments or did they slip by you and you didn't recognize them till you experienced this exercise? If you discovered fear gripped your day, what can you do to maintain a love based connection throughout the day? Incorporate this exercise into your journaling experience for the next seven days. Doing so will force you to consciously work with God/the Universe instead of unconsciously allowing random unsupervised thoughts to create your day.

JOURNAL PAGE:

DAY ONE:

DAY TWO:

DAY THREE:

DAY FOUR:

DAY FIVE:

DAY SIX:

DAY SEVEN:

My discoveries:

EXTERNAL INHARMONY

Florence states that "As man becomes spiritually awakened he recognizes that any external in-harmony is the correspondence of the mental inharmony."

We've learned that we vibrate at the frequency of our internal beliefs and thought patterns. The universe then matches to us that of the same vibration in love, health, wealth and perfect self-expression.

WORKBOOK ITEM SIX

The external of your life will reflect what is going on inside of you. Are you living the life you desire?

Review your life – are you in harmony in each of area of your Square of Life? If not, look within. What is the root of the inharmony? Use the Healing Circle of Love to shift to love within in order to attract to you what you truly desire and shift to a harmonious state of love internally and externally.

Square of Life Make Believe/Visualization Form

Health – A healthy physical body that houses our spirit
Love - Relationships that are fulfilling and love based

Perfect Self-Expression – Work that fulfills our passion that we love

Wealth – Cash flow that fulfills our needs and desires

Use the Journal Page to write about your experience in shifting your internal affairs to reflect the life you wish to live externally.

JOUNRL PAGE:

NO LOSS IN DIVINE MIND

In Divine Mind/God/The Universal Supply Warehouse, there is no loss.

Man believes in loss. Again, loss is a fear based, negative thought and emotion. It is up to us, as spiritual beings to release the emotions of loss and transmute them to forgiveness and non-resistance.

When we reach a state of forgiveness and non-resistance, there is no loss in our mind. Therefore, we are at a place of creating our desire. Florence's example is of the woman who had lost $2,000.00 in loaning it to a relative who died before the loan was repaid.

Florence taught the woman to forgive the loss and become non-resistant; she was then able to claim as hers, the $2,000.00. She raised her vibrational frequency to one of love base – full of gratitude for there was no loss, no fear – and she received.

The Bank of the Universe has an unlimited amount of withdrawal slips and this woman learned how to fill one out!

MAN: THE GIVER AND THE TAKER

Maintaining fear based thought patterns and beliefs rob us of our birthright – a life of abundance in all areas of our life – health, wealth, love and perfect self-expression. There is no way to experience Joy in these areas while living in a state that is fear based for there is no room for fear in Joy and no room for Joy in fear.

The Master Teachers who have walked the earth have tried to teach us that we are one with God. In being one with God we inherently possess His ability to create. Therefore, we have the power to bring to fruition the desires of our heart.

As Florence states, "no man give to himself, but himself, and no man takes away from himself, but himself." Through an understanding of Universal Laws we now understand that we are the creators of our reality – we are the creators of lack or blocks and we are the creators of receiving.

The environment we live in is a creation of our focus, of our thought patterns and beliefs. By working in tandem with the conscious, subconscious and the superconscious to maintain our thought patterns and beliefs as well as words and action in a love base, we culminate our emotions and feelings into a life of abundance and prosperity.

It is our choice.

WORKBOOK ITEM SEVEN

Do you have a life situation, event or relationship that causes you pain from feelings of loss? Using Florence's examples of denying loss, write your own treatment:

Treatment Form

I deny loss, there is no loss in Divine Mind, therefore:

RECAP

Getting our mind around the teachings of Ms Shinn is, indeed, a challenge. But once we are able to grasp the depth of her world, all becomes clear. We are able to see how our thought patterns and beliefs have shaped our lives.

We create the status of our relationships, finances, health and our work. We do it.

We are taught by the physical world to blame others – to be a victim. We are not victims. We are choosing – daily – what we want our lives to be.

Knowing this to be true, we are then better able to accept the fact that we can truly BE, HAVE and DO anything we desire.

Florence Scovel Shinn was and is a truly gifted spirit whose life was an example to all she came into contact with. You too, will be an example of Florence's teachings – working in tandem with the conscious, subconscious and superconscious minds – working as one with God/The Universal Supply Warehouse. People will be asking how you did it!

In looking back at your life since you opened this workbook, you can see how your life has changed. As you have experienced these pages it is clear to see that all is not as it seems in many situations. A seeming adversity may be the stepping stone to fulfillment of our highest good – of what we desire. We've learned to bless adversity for in so doing, we become based in love forcing the Universe to "match" to us – more love. You can see the growth in the experiences expressed in your journal. Ascension is a gift and you are experiencing it.

Continue to journal – daily if you possibly can. Your journal is a direct gateway to connecting with God and maintaining balance of your three levels of consciousness. It always will be. Daily journaling will bring forward more and more information, more understanding, and more spiritual growth.

Be sure to thank your guides, teachers and angels for being in attendance and helping you to clearly understand God's work.

May you be profoundly blessed in this moment and in every moment after…

JOURNAL PAGES:

JOURNAL PAGES continued:

"No wind can drive my bark astray nor change the tide of destiny."

There is for each man, perfect self-expression. There is a place which he is to fill and no one else can fill, something which he is to do, which no one else can do; it is his destiny!

This achievement is held, a perfect idea in Divine Mind, awaiting man's recognition. As the imaging faculty is the creative faculty, it is necessary for man to see the idea, before it can manifest.

So man's highest demand is for the *Divine Design of his life.*

He may not have the faintest conception of what it is, for there is, possibly, some marvelous talent, hidden deep within him.

His demand should be: *"Infinite Spirit, open the way for the Divine Design of my life to manifest; let the genius within me now be released; let me see clearly the perfect plan."*

The perfect plan includes health, wealth, love and perfect self-expression. This is the *square of life,* which brings perfect happiness. When one has made this demand, he may find great changes taking place in his life, for nearly every man has wandered far from the Divine Design.

I know, in one woman's case, it was as though a cyclone had struck her affairs, but readjustments came quickly, and new and wonderful conditions took the place of old ones.

Perfect self-expression will never be labor; but of such absorbing interest that it will seem almost like play. The student knows, also, as man comes into the world financed by God, the *supply* needed for his perfect self-expression will be at hand.

Many a genius has struggled for years with the problem of supply, when his spoken word, and faith, would have released quickly, the necessary funds.

For example: After the class, one day, a man came to me and handed me a cent.

He said: "I have just seven cents in the world, and I'm going to give you one; for I have faith in the power of your spoken word. I want you to speak the word for my perfect self-expression and prosperity."

I "spoke the word," and did not see him again until a year later. He came in one day, successful and happy, with a roll of yellow bills in his pocket. He said, "Immediately after you spoke the word, I had a position offered me in a distant city, and am now demonstrating health, happiness and supply."

A woman's perfect self-expression may be in becoming a perfect wife, a perfect mother, a perfect home-maker and not necessarily in having a public career.

Demand definite leads, and the way will be made easy and successful.

One should not visualize or force a mental picture. When he demands the Divine Design to come into his conscious mind, he will receive flashes of inspiration, and begin to see himself making some great accomplishment. This is the picture, or idea, he must hold without wavering.

The thing man seeks is seeking him - *the telephone was seeking Bell!*

Parents should never force careers and professions upon their children. With a knowledge of spiritual Truth, the Divine Plan could be spoken for, early in childhood, or prenatally.

A prenatal treatment should be: "Let the God in this child have perfect expression; let the Divine Design of his mind, body and affairs be made manifest throughout his life, throughout eternity."

God's will be done, not man's; God's pattern, not man's pattern, is the command we find running through all the scriptures, and the Bible is a book dealing with the science of the mind. It is a book telling man how to release his soul (or subconscious mind) from bondage.

The battles described are pictures of man waging war against mortal thoughts. "A man's foes shall be they of his own household." Every man is Jehoshaphat, and every man is David, who slays Goliath (mortal thinking) with the little white stone (faith).

So man must be careful that his is not the "wicked and slothful servant" who buried his talent. There is a terrible penalty to be paid for not using one's ability.

Often fear stands between man and his perfect self-expression. Stage-fright has hampered many a genius. This may be overcome by the spoken word or treatment. The individual then loses all self-consciousness, and feels simply that he is a channel for Infinite Intelligence to express Itself through.

He is under direct inspiration, fearless, and confident; for he feels that it is the "Father within" him who does the work.

A young boy came often to my class with his mother. He asked me to "speak the word" for his coming examinations at school.

I told him to make the statement: "I am one with Infinite Intelligence. I know everything I should know on this subject." He had an excellent knowledge of history, but was not sure of his arithmetic. I saw him afterwards, and he said: "I spoke the word for my arithmetic, and passed with the highest honors; but thought I could depend on myself for history, and got a very poor mark." Man often receives a set-back when he is "too sure of himself," which means he is trusting to his personality and not the "Father within."

Another one of my students gave me an example of this. She took an extended trip abroad one summer, visiting many countries, where she was ignorant of the languages. She was calling for guidance and protection every minute, and her affairs went smoothly and miraculously. Her luggage was never delayed nor lost! Accommodations were always ready for her at the best hotels; and she had perfect service wherever she went. She returned to New York. Knowing the language, she felt God was no longer necessary, so looked after her affairs in an ordinary manner.

Everything went wrong, her trunks delayed, amid inharmony and confusion. The student must form the habit of "practicing the Presence of God" every minute. *"In all thy ways acknowledge him;"* nothing is too small or too great.

Sometimes an insignificant incident may be the turning point in a man's life.

Robert Fulton, watching some boiling water, simmering in a tea kettle, saw a steamboat!

I have seen a student, often, keep back his demonstration, through resistance, or pointing the way.

He pins his faith to one channel only, and dictates just the way he desires the manifestation to come, which brings things to a standstill.

"My way, not your way!" is the command of Infinite Intelligence. Like all Power, be it steam or electricity, it must have a non-resistant engine or instrument to work through, and man is that engine or instrument. Over and over again, man is told to "stand still". "Oh Judah, fear not; but to-morrow go out against them, for the lord will be with you. You shall not need to fight this battle; set yourselves, stand ye still, and see the salvation of the Lord with you."

We see this in the incidents of the two thousand dollars coming to the woman through the landlord when she became *non-resistant* and *undisturbed*, and the woman who won the man's love "after all suffering had ceased."

The student's goal is *Poise! Poise* is *Power*, for it gives God-Power a chance to rush through man, to "will and to do Its good pleasure."

Poised, he thinks clearly, and makes "right decisions quickly." "He never misses a trick."

Anger blurs the visions, poisons the blood, is the root of many diseases, and causes wrong decision leading to failure.

It has been named one of the worst "sins," as its reaction is so harmful. The student learns that in metaphysics sin has a much broader meaning than in the old teaching. "Whatsoever is not of faith is sin."

He finds that fear and worry are deadly sins. They are inverted faith, and through distorted mental pictures, bring to pass the thing he fears. His work is to drive out these enemies (from the subconscious mind). "When Man is *fearless he is finished!*" Maeterlinck says, that "Man is God afraid."

So as we read in the previous chapters; man can only vanquish fear by walking up to the thing he is afraid of. When Jehoshaphat and his army prepared to meet the enemy, singing "Praise the Lord, for his mercy endureth forever," they found their enemies had destroyed each other, and there was nothing to fight.

For example: A woman asked a friend to deliver a message to another friend. The woman feared to give the message, as the reasoning mind said, "Don't get mixed-up in this affair, don't give that message."

She was troubled in spirit, for she had given her promise. At last, she determined to "walk up to the lion," and call on the law of divine protection. She met the friend to whom she was to deliver the message. She opened her mouth to speak it, when her friend said, "So and So has left town," This made it unnecessary to give the message, as the situation depended upon the person being in town. As she was willing to do it, she was not obliged to; as she did not fear, the situation vanished.

The student often delays his demonstration through a belief in incompletion. He should make this statement:

"In Divine Mind there is only completion, therefore, my demonstration is completed. My perfect work, my perfect home, my perfect health." Whatever he demands are perfect ideas registered in Divine Mind, and must manifest, "under grace in a perfect way." He gives thanks he has already received on the invisible, and makes active preparation for receiving on the visible.

One of my students was in need of a financial demonstration. She came to me and asked why it was not completed.

I replied: "Perhaps, you are in the habit of leaving things unfinished, and the subconscious has gotten into the habit of not completing (as the without, so the within)."

She said, "you are right. I often *begin things* and never finish them."

"I'll go home and finish something I commenced weeks ago, and I know it will be symbolic of my demonstration."

She sewed assiduously, and the article was soon completed. Shortly after, the money came in a most curious manner.

Her husband was paid his salary twice that month. He told the people of their mistake, and they sent word to keep it.

When man ask, *believing, he must receive, for God creates His own channels!*

I have been sometimes asked, "Suppose one has several talents, how is he to know which one to choose?"

Demand to be shown definitely, Say: "Infinite Spirit, give me a definite lead, reveal to me my perfect self-expression, show me which talent I am to make use of now."

I have known people to suddenly enter a new line of work, and be fully equipped, with little or no training. So make the statement: *"I am fully equipped for the Divine Plan of my life,"* and be fearless in grasping opportunities.

Some people are cheerful givers, but bad receivers. They refuse gifts through pride, or some negative reason, thereby blocking their channels, and invariably find themselves eventually with little or nothing. For example: A woman who had given away a great deal of money, had a gift offered her of several thousand dollars. She refused to take it, saying she did not need it. Shortly after that, her finances were "tied up", and she found herself in debt for that amount. Man should receive gracefully the bread returning to him upon the water – freely ye have given, freely ye shall receive.

There is always the perfect balance of giving and receiving, and though man should give without thinking of returns, he violates law if he does not accept the returns which come to him; for all gifts are from God, man being merely the channel.

A thought of lack should never be held over the giver.

For example: When the man gave the one cent, I did not say; "Poor man, he cannot afford to give me that." I saw him rich and prosperous, with his supply pouring in. It was this thought which brought it. If one has been a bad receiver, he must become a good one, and take even a postage stamp if it is given him, and open up his channels for receiving.

The Lord loveth a cheerful receiver, as well as a cheerful giver.

I have often been asked why one man is born rich and healthy, and another poor and sick.

Where there is an effect there is always a cause; there is no such thing as chance.

This question is answered through the law of reincarnation. Man goes through many births and deaths, until he knows the truth which sets him free.

He is drawn back to the earth plane through unsatisfied desire, to pay his Karmic debts, or to "fulfill his destiny."

The man born rich and healthy has had pictures in his subconscious mind, in his past life, of health and riches; and the poor and sick man, of disease and poverty. Man manifests, on any plane, the sum total of his subconscious beliefs.

However, birth and death are man-made laws, for the "wages of sin is death"; the Adamic fall in consciousness through the belief in *two powers*. The real man, spiritual man, is birthless and deathless! He never was born and has never died - "As he was in the beginning, he is now, and ever shall be!"

So through the truth, man is set free from the law of Karma, sin and death, and manifests the man made in "His image and likeness." Man's freedom comes through fulfilling his destiny, bringing into manifestation the Divine Design of his life.

His lord will say unto him: "Well done thou good and faithful servant, thou has been faithful over a few things, I will make thee ruler over many things (death itself); enter thou into in the joy of thy Lord (eternal life)."

Workbook Session Nine - Expression or the Divine Design

In this session:

- Divine Life Path
- Financed by God
- Demanding Leads/Asking for Guidance
- God's Will Not Man's
- Man as a Non-Resistant Instrument
- Fear and Worry
- The Cheerful Receiver – Balance of Giving and Receiving
- Recap and Journal Pages

Begin this session by asking Archangel Michael to surround you with God's Divine White Light of Protection and set your intention to connect with your higher self – the God part within.

Father, Mother, God, Creator of All That Is...

I claim my personal power and open the way to see clearly my field of potentiality, my field of infinite possibilities. I cut the ties of beliefs and thought patterns that no longer serve me in all directions of time thereby removing them from my consciousness, my subconscious and my superconscious. I fearlessly step into the magnificence of the true essence of who I am – One with God. I graciously accept all that is mine by divine right, under grace in a miraculous way and commit to fulfill all that I came to be, have and do in this incarnation on Mother Earth at this time.

Amen

Ask your guides, angels and teachers to be present with you to help you open your heart, mind and spirit to the infinite possibilities.

What would your life look like if you believed you were financed by God?

DIVINE LIFE PATH

Each one of us is a uniquely gifted spiritual being. We are the only one who can fill our space in the physical world of earth. Each one of us has purpose and a mission to fulfill. Each one of us asks, "What is my mission? What is my Divine Life Path?"

Florence tells us to demand: *"Infinite Spirit, open the way for the Divine Design of my life to manifest; let the genius within me now be released; let me see clearly the perfect plan."*

We learned in Chapter Eight, Intuition and Guidance, that when we demand from God/The Universal Supply Warehouse, we make a formal claim to what is ours as our birthright. We've also learned how to work in tandem, as one, with the conscious, subconscious and superconscious. We now know how to look within to the God Part within us and how to discern the guidance of that God Part, our intuition.

Florence has given us the tools necessary to bring into our reality our highest good in all areas of our square of life – health, wealth, love, and perfect self-expression.

We've learned how to connect with the God Part within, our intuition, and in so doing have a direct connection with God.

WORKBOOK ITEM ONE

This exercise is designed to help you discern your location in our Divine Life Path. Sit quietly and breathe deeply and completely.

Allow the chatter of the physical world to melt away. If random thoughts flitter in, acknowledge them and bless them on their way. Set the intention to connect with your God Part within and use the Sacred Space ~ Build It and They Will Come meditation.

Connect with your God Part and honestly review your life path. What you have been doing and what you desire to do.

Each time you experience this connection you will learn more about yourself and the path of your life. Use the Journal Page to write about your experiences and your developing life path. Be honest in your writings.

JOURNAL PAGE:

FINANCED BY GOD

Physical world conditioning teaches us that we are limited by circumstances, environment, race, cultures and locality. We are only truly limited if we believe this conditioning.

In reality we are gifted, limitless spiritual beings experiencing a human existence. As profoundly loved children of God our birthright is to live in prosperous abundance in all areas of our lives. It is our birthright.

In 1988 four men from Jamaica and their coach entered the Olympic Winter Games in Calvary. They entered the Bobsledding Event. There is no snow in Jamaica to practice bobsledding. The physical world, practical mind would tell us their entering the event was absurd. However, they qualified and they raced. In the 1992 Winter Olympics the team finished 14th, stunning their critics. In 1993 Disney immortalized the original Jamaican Bobsledding Team through the movie *"Cool Runnings."*

We are *Limitless Spiritual Beings…*

Florence teaches us that the world is financed by God. God is The Universal Supply Warehouse – the All That Is. She also teaches us that our *"perfect self-expression,"* our work, *"will never be labor; but of such absorbing interest that it will seem almost like play."* When we *love* what we do our work *is like play!*

In following our guidance to our perfect self-expression we may be led to surprising locations, services, etc. But when we follow these leads, these hunches, our intuition, we find our true happiness and joy in the work, the service that we give to the world. In working with our conscious, subconscious and superconscious, we also discover that monies needed to further our education, move us to a new location, the money to support us is provided – often times miraculously.

Our lives are financed by God, the Universal Supply Warehouse. We make the choice whether to believe we *are limitless beings* and to trust and experience faith in God/the Universal Supply Warehouse and receive abundance in our square of life or to believe physical world conditioning that we are limited.

WORKBOOK ITEM TWO

This exercise is designed to once again bring to your conscious mind how truly limitless you are. Read the question carefully; look within. Allow yourself to experience your connection with God and dream big.

Dream Session

What would your life look like if all areas of your life were filled with abundance – your health, your love, your finances and your work – what would your life look like? What would you look like? Who would you be with? How much money would you have and where would you work? Write your answers below:

Use the Journal Page to write about your thoughts of this exercise. What can you do today to bring into your reality, the life of your dreams?

Remember: If you can dream it, *it is* in your Field of Potentiality!

JOURNAL PAGE:

DEMANDING LEADS/ASKING FOR GUIDANCE

We have the choice to struggle and flail around in our physical world life on our own or to work with God/the Universe to create the life we really desire.

Every Day we make choices. We choose to live our lives from a source of fear or a source of love. Every day we make this choice. The physical world is full of pitfalls, tests, trials and challenges. It is what we do with these challenges that define who we are. It is the wise spiritual being who demands, formally claims leads/guidance. The guidance is ours, all we have to do is connect with it, open our heart to understand it, and then act on it.

WORKBOOK ITEM THREE

This exercise is designed to take up where the last exercise left off. Read the question carefully, and then allow yourself to connect with your God Part within. After you have pondered and chatted with your God Part write what you discovered.

What can I do today to bring the life of my dreams into my reality?

What can I do this week to bring the life of my dreams into reality?

What can I do this month to bring the life of my dreams into reality?

What can I do this year to bring the life of my dreams into reality?

What would I do if I knew I could not fail?

Notice the questions are "what can I do?" not "how do I?", but "what can I do?" Of course you'll need to really discern what it is that you desire. And you may want to work on one area of your life at a time so as not to overwhelm yourself. Use the Journal Page to write about how you felt doing this exercise. Did the life of your dreams become more real? Were you able to achieve a feeling of gratitude of receipt?

JOURNAL PAGE:

GOD'S WILL NOT MAN'S

Florence explains to us that *"A man's foes shall be they of his own household."* The foes are man's fears within himself. We choose to fear or not to fear.

Fear is an awkward motivator to most of our actions, thoughts and words. When we research it fully, there is no basis for fear, therefore the lives based in fear crumble unhappily – fear is an illusion.

When man aligns his thinking, words and actions with Love, with God, he can only prosper. God has a complete picture of our lives – of what our highest good really is. In Divine Mind, there is no fear, only love. In basing our lives in love, our thoughts, words and actions, we align ourselves with God's will. Remember, all thoughts, words and actions are either based in love or fear – there is no in between.

As we learn more through Florence's work, we see the logical sequence of events as we grow. Transmuting our fear based emotions, thought patterns and beliefs, words and actions to ones of love, moves us to become One with God, to trust and have faith in His ability to care for us and to provide for us as the universal supply. We discover that we are not alone in this physical world, for we are indeed a powerful force, a creator along with God to bring love and goodness to the world.

However, we are living a human experience and there will be times that we allow the physical world to come between us and God. When this happens, we will see clearly, distinctly the fear based thoughts, words and actions creeping back into our daily routine. Our vibrational frequency level will, if we allow, lower back to fear base. We will then again, become a magnet for fear based things to come to us.

God's will is based in love, when our will is based in love, then we merge together as One with God.

WORKBOOK ITEM FOUR

This exercise is again designed to evaluate your square of life. Read each question and evaluate the feelings that stir within you. Are they love based or fear based? Are you working in tandem with the three levels of consciousness? Working as one with God/the Universe? Evaluate this honestly and write your findings.

Square of Life Today Form

Health – A healthy physical body that houses our spirit

Love - Relationships that are fulfilling and love based

Perfect Self-Expression – Work that fulfills our passion that we love

Wealth – Cash flow that fulfills our needs and desires

Did you discover that you are, indeed, working with God and the three levels of consciousness or did you find weak areas? Use the tools you have learned to eliminate weakness and eradicate fear. Use the Journal Page to write about your discoveries and what you will do to become One with God.

JOURNAL PAGE:

MAN AS A NON-RESISTANT INSTRUMENT

God is our supply in all things – including the air that we breathe. We don't worry that there will be enough air – it isn't a concern. We don't try to control it; the air simply flows around us and in us through our breath. We are non-resistant to the air.

As Humans, we have a tendency to want to "control" everything. This need to control events, conditions, situations and people around us puts up a wall of resistance. This resistance blocks universal flow. Resistance is a negative, fear based action/emotion.

Florence teaches us to become a non-resistant instrument, to allow God to work through us. Achieving this state of trust and faith not only unlocks the doors of abundance for each area of our life, it will nail it open!

The example Florence used of the woman who was traveling abroad shows us that while the woman was working in tandem with God, trusting that God would be her supply, she was non-resistant. Her non-resistance allowed God/the Universe, to provide for her. The moment she took control of her affairs, she put up a wall of resistance, thereby stopping the flow of God's supply.

Becoming a non-resistant instrument allows the universe to flow freely our supply to us, around us and through us –as with the air that surrounds us.

In setting the intent to be non-resistant to the events, conditions, situations and people around us, we base ourselves in love – as One with God. We exhibit that we are trusting and in faith of God's wisdom. As a result, we are able to think clearly to discern our next action without the hindrance of fear based emotions of resistance getting in our way.

Being non-resistant does NOT mean that we do not care. The act of non-resistance is our trust and faith in God as our supply.

FEAR AND WORRY

Fear and worry are as thieves in the night robbing us of our abundance, our health, our love, our perfect work, and our cash flow.

We've learned that anger, fear, worry, unforgiveness – all fear based thoughts, words and actions will create disease and illness in the body.

Fear based thoughts, words and actions will destroy our love relationships.

Fear based thoughts, words and actions will block us from our perfect work.

Fear based thoughts, words and actions will stall cash flow.

So, what does fear and worry do to enhance our lives? *Nothing.* The actions, words and thoughts of fear and worry make us a magnet for more of the fear and worry.

Florence shows us by example how facing our fear will dissipate it – will cause it to vanish.

Through the teachings of this workbook, we have learned to identify those feelings of fear and worry that in the beginning were "normal" feelings. We now recognize that through physical world teachings, fear and worry are normal. But now, we know that living in fear and worry is a choice and it is *NOT* normal.

WORKBOOK ITEM FIVE

This exercise is designed to identify any lingering fears that have been hiding or have returned. Remember, you are living in a physical world surrounded by fear and negativity. Rewriting your subconscious CD takes time. Be gentle with yourself and simply release the fears and realign yourself with love as your source.

Revisit any new layers of fear revealed to you in the previous exercise. Use the Sedona Method® of Release or the Healing Circle of Love to transmute the fear to love. Use the Journal Page to write about your experience.

JOURNAL PAGE:

THE CHEERFUL RECEIVER – BALANCE OF GIVING AND RECEIVING

Florence tells us *"Man should receive gracefully the bread returning to him upon the water – freely ye have given, freely ye shall receive. There is always the perfect balance of giving and receiving, and though man should give without thinking of returns, he violates law if he does not accept the returns which come to him; for all gifts are from God, man being merely the channel."*

Receiving cheerfully, with love, is as important as giving cheerfully, with love. As we learned previously, being non-resistant opens our doors to abundance. If we deny or turn down someone giving to us, we effectively block our receipt - the flow of universal supply.

Florence gives the example of accepting the penny from the man who had only seven cents to his name. She did not see him as a poor man, but as a rich and prosperous man – and so he was. Had she denied his gift to her she would not only have stopped his flow, but hers as well.

Graciously and cheerfully receive what the universe sends to you. This is your part in the flow of universal abundance to not only yourself, but to others. None of us want to be the block for someone else – practice gracious, cheerful receiving!

WORKBOOK ITEM SIX

This exercise is designed to discover if you are a cheerful receiver! Read each question carefully and answer it honestly.

1. You receive a check in the mail for $1.50 – do you cash it or throw it away?

2. A friend says to you, I only have $2 to my name for the week and I want to give you $1 – do you accept it graciously or tell them to keep it?

3. A neighbor comes by your house with two jars of peanut butter that she doesn't need and you love peanut butter – do you accept it graciously or send her on her way with the peanut butter?

4. You have lunch with a friend and they offer to pay for lunch – do you graciously accept or insist on paying for your half?

Each of these events are gifts from the universe – any time we are in receipt of something, it is a gift from the universe. To encourage universal flow of abundance, the answer is to graciously accept each gift. Use the Journal Page to write about any past examples of being a gracious receiver.

JOURNAL PAGE:

RECAP

What does fear and worry do to enhance my life?

This question is a real eye opener.

Living a life in fear and worry is a choice.

This statement is heart wrenching.

What we continually focus on will manifest in our lives.

This question and these statements together are life changing.

Clearly, you've made the decision to live from a love base – you have continued the workbook. In all probability, you have experienced profound changes in your life since opening it. Incorporating love based thought patterns and beliefs into your conscious, subconscious and superconscious has changed your life.

Hasn't it?

Now you notice when fear creeps in and you take the necessary steps to transmute it to love. You like this new way of living, consciously attracting what you really want into your life instead of unconsciously living in whatever you happen to be focusing on at the time.

You can't go back. Now you have a firm grasp on the laws of the universe, the concept of God within us, working together as One and how to work *with* God to bring to fruition the true desires of your heart – fulfilling your true Divine Life Path.

There are times that tragedies affect an area and people die in mass. For some it was a chosen way to exit the physical world, for others, their vibrational frequency magnetized the event to them. Their vibrational frequency was of the same vibrational frequency of the traumatic event and they became involved in it.

In Florence's teachings we now understand this. We have learned to maintain a higher frequency of love based thoughts.

The physical world can be a harsh place, yet with this blossoming of inner knowing; it is easier to focus on the beauty and the love that the physical world can offer. As we focus on these love based thought patterns, beliefs, words and actions, we attract and bring forth yet more love. Through our love, one person at a time, the world will find peace and tranquility.

Your journal is a priceless tool of support and guidance to help you stay on track. Yes, all this changing can be accomplished without it, but the changes are much easier with the aid of the journal. Write in your journal daily, life will be easier!

Be sure to thank your guides, teachers and angels for being in attendance and helping you to clearly understand God's work and guidance.

May you be profoundly blessed in this moment and in every moment after…

JOURNAL PAGE:

"Thou shalt decree a thing, and it shall be established unto thee."

All the good that is to be made manifest in man's life is already an accomplished fact in divine mind, and is released through man's recognition, or spoken word, so he must be careful to decree that only the Divine Idea be made manifest, for often, he decrees, through his "idle words," failure or misfortune.

It is, therefore, of the utmost importance, to word one's demands correctly, as stated in a previous chapter.

If one desires a home, friend, position or any other good thing, make the demand for the "divine selection."

For example: "Infinite Spirit, open the way for my right home, my right friend, my right position. I give thanks *it now manifests under grace in a perfect way.*"

The latter part of the statement is most important. For example: I knew a woman who demanded a thousand dollars. Her daughter was injured and they received a thousand dollars indemnity, so it did not come in a "perfect way."

The demand should have been worded in this way: "Infinite Spirit, I give thanks that the one thousand dollars, which is mine by divine right, is now released, and reaches me under grace in a perfect way."

As one grows in a financial consciousness, he should demand that the enormous sums of money, which are his by divine right, reach him under grace, in perfect ways.

It is impossible for man to release more than he thinks is possible, for one is bound by the limited expectancies of the subconscious. He must enlarge his expectancies in order to receive in a larger way.

Man so often limits himself in his demands. For example: A student made the demand for six hundred dollars, by a certain date. He did receive it, but heard afterwards, that he came very near receiving a thousand dollars, but he was given just six hundred, as the result of his spoken word.

"They limited the Holy One of Isreal." Wealth is a matter of consciousness. The French have a legend giving an example of this. A poor man was walking along a road when he met a traveler, who stopped him and said: "My good friend, I see you are poor. Take this gold nugget, sell it, and you will be rich all your days."

The man was overjoyed at his good fortune, and took the nugget home. He immediately found work and became so prosperous that he did not sell the nugget. Years passed, and he became a very rich man. One day he met a poor man on the road. He stopped him and said: "My good friend, I will give you this gold nugget, which, if you sell, will make you rich for life." The mendicant took the nugget, had it valued, and found it was only brass. So we see, the first man became rich through feeling rich, thinking the nugget was gold.

Every man has within himself a gold nugget; *it is his consciousness of gold, of opulence, which brings riches into his life.* In making his demands, man begins at his *journey's end,* that is he declares *he has already received. "Before* ye call I shall answer."

Continually affirming establishes the belief in the subconscious.

It would not be necessary to make an affirmation more than once if one had perfect faith! One should not plead or supplicate, but give thanks repeatedly, that he has received.

"The desert shall rejoice and blossom as the rose." This rejoicing which is yet in the desert (state of consciousness) opens the way for release. The Lord's Prayer is in the form of command and demand, "Give us this day our daily bread, and forgive us our debts as we forgive our debtors," and ends in praise, "For thine is the Kingdom and the Power and the Glory, forever. Amen." "Concerning the works of my hands, command ye me." So prayer is command and demand, praise and thanksgiving. The student's work is in making himself believe that "with God all things are possible."

This is easy enough to state in the abstract, but a little more difficult when confronted with a problem. For example: It was necessary for a woman to demonstrate a large sum of money within a stated time. She knew she must *do something* to get a realization (for realization is manifestation), and she demanded a "lead."

She was walking through a department store, when she saw a very beautiful pink enamel papercutter. She felt the "pull" towards it. The thought came. "I haven't a paper cutter good enough to open letters containing large cheques."

So she bought the papercutter, which the reasoning mind would have called an extravagance. When she held it in her hand, she had a flash of a picture of herself opening an envelope containing a large cheque, and in a few weeks, she received the money. The pink papercutter was her bridge of active faith.

Many stories are told of the power of the subconscious when directed in faith.

For example: A man was spending the night in a farmhouse. The windows of the room had been nailed down, and in the middle of the night he felt suffocated and made his way in the dark to the window. He could not open it, so he smashed the pane with his fist, drew in draughts of fine fresh air, and had a wonderful night's sleep.

The next morning, he found he had smashed the glass of a bookcase and the window had remained closed during the whole night. He had *supplied himself with oxygen, simply by his thought of oxygen.*

When a student starts out to demonstrate, he should never turn back. "Let not that man who wavers think that he shall receive anything of the Lord."

A student once made this wonderful statement, "When I ask the Father for anything, I put my foot down, and I say: Father, I'll take nothing less than I've asked for, but more!" So man should never compromise: "Having done all - Stand." This is sometimes the most difficult time of demonstrating. The temptation comes to give up, to turn back, to compromise.

"He also serves who only stands and waits."

Demonstrations often come at the eleventh hour because man then lets go, that is, stops reasoning, and Infinite Intelligence has a chance to work.

"Man's dreary desires are answered drearily, and his impatient desires, long delayed or violently fulfilled.

For example: A woman asked me why it was she was constantly losing or breaking her glasses.

We found she often said to herself and others with vexation, "I wish I could get rid of my glasses." So her impatient desire was violently fulfilled. What she should have demanded was perfect eye-sight, but what she registered in the subconscious was simply the impatient desire to be rid of her glasses; so they were continually being broken or lost.

Two attitudes of mind cause loss: depreciation, as in the case of the woman who did not appreciate her husband, *or fear of loss*, which makes a picture of loss in the subconscious.

When a student is able to let go of his problem (cast his burden) he will have instantaneous manifestation.

For example: A woman was out during a very stormy day and her umbrella was blown inside-out. She was about to make a call on some people whom she had never met and she did not wish to make her first appearance with a dilapidated umbrella. She could not throw it away, as it did not belong to her. So in desperation, she exclaimed: "Oh God, you take charge of this umbrella, I don't know what to do."

A moment later, a voice behind her said: "Lady, do you want your umbrella mended? There stood an umbrella mender.

She replied, "Indeed, I do."

The man mended the umbrella, while she went into the house to pay her call, and when she returned, she had a good umbrella. So there is always an umbrella mender at hand, on man's pathway, when one puts the umbrella (or situation) in God's Hands.

One should always follow a denial with an affirmation.

For example: I was called on the 'phone late one night to treat a man whom I had never seen. He was apparently very ill. I made the statement: "I deny this appearance of disease. It is unreal, therefore cannot register in his consciousness; this man is a perfect idea in Divine Mind, pure substance expressing perfection."

There is no time or space, in Divine Mind, therefore the word reaches instantly its destination and does not "return void." I have treated patients in Europe and have found that the result was instantaneous.

I am asked so often the difference between visualizing and visioning. Visualizing is a mental process governed by the reasoning or conscious mind; visioning is a spiritual process, governed by intuition, or the superconscious mind. The student should train his mind to receive these flashes of inspiration, and work out the "divine pictures," through definite leads. When a man can say, "I desire only that which God desires for me," his new set of blueprints is given him by the Master Architect, the God within. God's plan for each man transcends the limitation of the reasoning mind, and is always the square of life, containing health, wealth, love and perfect self-expression. Many a man is building for himself in imagination a bungalow when he should be building a palace.

If a student tries to force a demonstration (through the reasoning mind) he brings it to a standstill. "I will hasten it," saith the Lord. He should act only through intuition, or definite leads. "Rest in the Lord and wait patiently.

Trust also in him, and he will bring it to pass."

I have seen the law work in the most astonishing manner. For example: A student stated that it was necessary for her to have a hundred dollars for the following day. It was a debt of vital importance which had to be met. I "spoke the word," declaring Spirit was "never too late" and that the supply was at hand.

That evening she phoned me of the miracle. She said that the thought came to her to go to her safe-deposit box at the bank to examine some papers. She looked over the papers, and at the bottom of the box, was a new one hundred dollar bill. She was astounded, and said she knew she had never put it there, for she had gone through the papers many times. It may have been a materialization, as Jesus Christ materialized the loaves and fishes.

Man will reach the stage where his "word is made flesh," or materialized, instantly. "The fields, ripe with the harvest," will manifest immediately, as in all of the miracles of Jesus Christ.

There is a tremendous power alone in the name Jesus Christ. It stands for *Truth Made Manifest.* He said, "Whatsoever ye ask the Father, in my name, he will give it to you."

The power of this name raises the student into the fourth dimension, where he is freed from all astral and psychic influences, and he becomes "unconditioned and absolute, as God Himself is unconditioned and absolute."

I have seen many healings accomplished by using the words, "In the name of Jesus Christ."

Christ was both person and principle; and the Christ within each man is his Redeemer and Salvation.

The Christ within, is his own fourth dimensional self, the man made in God's image and likeness. This is the self which has never failed, never known sickness or sorrow, was never born and has never died. It is the "resurrection and the life" of each man! "No man cometh to the Father save by the Son," means, that God, the Universal, working on the place of the particular, becomes the Christ in man; and the Holy Ghost, means God in-action. So daily, man is manifesting the Trinity of Father, Son and Holy Ghost.

Man should make an art of thinking. The Master Thinker is an artist and is careful to paint only the divine designs upon the canvas of his mind; and he paints these pictures with masterly strokes of power and decision, having perfect faith that there is no power to mar their perfection and that they shall manifest in his life the ideal made real.

All power is given man (through right thinking) to bring *his heaven* upon *his earth,* and this is the *goal of the "Game of Life."*

The simple rules are fearless faith, non-resistance and love!

May each reader be now freed from that thing which has held him in bondage through the ages, standing between him and his own, and "know the Truth which makes him free" - free to fulfill his destiny, to bring into manifestation the *"Divine Design of his life,* Health, Wealth, Love and Perfect Self-Expression." "Be ye transformed by the renewing of your mind."

Denials and Affirmations

For Prosperity: God is my unfailing supply, and large sums of money come to me quickly, under grace, in perfect ways.

For Right Conditions: Every plan my Father in heaven has not planned, shall be dissolved and dissipated, and the Divine Idea now comes to pass.

For Right Conditions: Only that which is true of God is true of me, for I and the Father are ONE.

For Faith: As I am one with God, I am one with my good, for God is both the *Giver* and the *Gift.* I cannot separate the Giver from the gift.

For Right Conditions: Divine Love now dissolves and dissipates every wrong condition in my mind, body and affairs. Divine Love is the most powerful chemical in the universe, and *dissolves everything* which is not of itself!

For Health: Divine Love floods my consciousness with health, and every cell in my body is filled with light.

For the Eyesight: My eyes are God's eyes, I see with the eyes of spirit. I see clearly the open way; there are no obstacles on my pathway. I see clearly the perfect plan.

For Guidance: I am divinely sensitive to my intuitive leads, and give instant obedience to Thy will.

For the Hearing: My ears are God's ears, I hear with the ears of spirit. I am non-resistant and am willing to be led I hear glad tidings of great joy.

For Right Work: I have a perfect work In a perfect way; I give a perfect service For perfect pay.

For Freedom from all Bondage: I cast this burden on the Christ within, and I go free!

In this session:

- Under Grace in a Perfect Way
- Limiting Thoughts and Beliefs vs Achieving a Feeling of Opulence
- Manifesting Fear Based Thoughts
- Releasing People/Conditions/Situations to God
- Visualizing and Visioning
- Rules: Fearless Faith, Non-resistance and Love!
- Recap and Journal Pages

Begin this session by asking Archangel Michael to surround you with God's Divine White Light of Protection and set your intention to connect with your higher self – the God part within.

Father, Mother, God, Creator of All That Is…

I claim my personal power and open the way to see clearly my field of potentiality, my field of infinite possibilities. I cut the ties of beliefs and thought patterns that no longer serve me in all directions of time thereby removing them from my consciousness, my subconscious and my superconscious. I fearlessly step into the magnificence of the true essence of who I am – One with God. I graciously accept all that is mine by divine right, under grace in a miraculous way and commit to fulfill all that I came to be, have and do in this incarnation on Mother Earth at this time.

Amen

Ask your guides, angels and teachers to be present with you to help you open your heart, mind and spirit to the infinite possibilities.

God's plan for each man transcends the limitation of the
reasoning mind, and is always the square of life containing
health, wealth, love and perfect self-expression.

UNDER GRACE IN A PERFECT WAY

We've learned that the Law of Attraction delivers to us that which we focus our attention through thought patterns and beliefs, words and actions.

Florence takes the application of this law a step further by teaching us to formally claim/demand, what is ours to come to us *"under grace in a perfect way."* Claiming what we desire in this way ensures that we are claiming our desire from a love base.

We've learned that all thoughts, words and actions are either love based or fear based – there is no in between. We've also learned that the Law of Attraction works for both love and fear. When we are living from a love source, we attract more love. When we are living from a fear source we attract more fear. The Universe makes no distinction as to whether our focus is love based or fear based – its job is to match to us the same vibrational frequency that we put out.

Therefore if we are not truly in a love base, if there is fear involved, what we desire may be matched to us from a fear base. This is how the woman who claimed formally/demanded $1,000 received it as an indemnity payment.

Demanding receipt *"under grace in a perfect way"* guarantees a love base.

LIMITING THOUGHTS AND BELIEFS vs ACHIEVING A FEELING OF OPULENCE

We've learned that the physical world conditions/teaches us to believe that we are limited in everything. Limited in what we can Be, Have, or Do. We've learned that the reality is that we are limitless spiritual beings that can Be, Have, or Do anything.

As we have elevated our vibrational frequency to a love based state, we have felt the feeling of opulence. It is easy for us to distinguish between the two – fear based limitedness and love based limitlessness/opulence. We have experienced the full spectrum – the lower vibrational frequency of fear and the higher vibrational frequency of love – we know what it feels like deep within our core.

Maintaining the feelings of opulence and love base takes repeated use of the tools and concepts learned here. Maintaining a life based in love is obtainable.

WORKBOOK ITEM ONE

This exercise is designed to help you recognize limiting thought patterns and beliefs when they happen so you may immediately change them from fear to love. Read the situation, and then recognize what your immediate feelings/thoughts are. Write them in the space.

Recognizing Sneaky Limiting/Fear Based Thoughts

1. Your car is at least 10 years old and has well over 100,000 miles on it. You've been admiring another newer model. You see an advertisement of the vehicle at a reduced price. Your immediate thought is:

a. I can't afford that.

b. I can have this vehicle!

2. You are in a relationship and you see two people snuggling (in an appropriate setting) your immediate thought is:

a. I never do that with my spouse/partner.

b. You experience a feeling of gratitude and love for your spouse/partner.

3. You are not in a relationship and you see two people snuggling (in an appropriate setting) your immediate thought is:

a. I'm always alone.

b. You feel the love and gratitude swell within your heart at the possibilities of your future!

4. A coworker gets an unexpected promotion – your immediate thought is:

a. Why doesn't anything good happen to me?

b. Your heart swells with happiness for the coworker!

5. You're walking down the street and the person behind you finds a $10 bill on the sidewalk. Your immediate thought is:

a. Why didn't I see that?

b. You feel joy for the good fortune of the person!

Use the Journal Page to write about what you discovered about yourself. Did you immediately think A or B consistently? If you chose A, please identify the basis for the negative reaction and work with the tools you have learned to release them. If you chose B, congratulations! You are living from a source of love!

JOURNAL PAGE:

MANIFESTING FEAR BASED THOUGHTS

We've learned of the power of our thoughts, beliefs, actions and words. We've also learned the power of the Law of Attraction.

As students of Florence Scovel Shinn, having read her book and now experienced this workbook, our ability to bring to fruition - manifest - what we focus on is even more powerful than it was before.

Each day as our minds waken to the day, we must consciously decide what our focus of the day will be. If we do not decide, our rambling thoughts will do it for us and we will be sending out unsupervised thoughts and feelings all day. We now know that the universe will then match to us whatever we have been thinking/focusing on.

In order to maintain the love based thoughts that we want to focus on we will use Attraction Magnets to move us back into a love base when fear and/or negativity sneak into our lives.

WORKBOOK ITEM TWO

This exercise is designed to create Gratitude Attraction Magnets. These Gratitude Attraction Magnets will be used when you recognize fear based thoughts interfering in your love based world. You'll be able to use these Attraction Magnets to transmute the fear based thoughts to love.

In previous exercises you have achieved a feeling of opulence by attaining a feeling of gratitude. You have attained the feelings of gratitude by focusing on things, people and situations you are grateful for. These things, people and situations are Gratitude Attraction Magnets.

List at least six things, people and situations (more if you can) that you feel opulently grateful for when you think about them.

Gratitude Attraction Magnets

1.

2.

3.

4.

5.

6.

7.

8.

9.

10.

Think of these Gratitude Attraction Magnets when you recognize fear based thoughts interfering in your love based world. Use the Journal Page to write about your experience in creating your Attraction Magnets. During the next week write in your journal each time you use them. Notice how quickly you are able to move from a fear based thought to a love based one by using one or several Gratitude Attraction Magnets.

JOURNAL PAGE:

RELEASING PEOPLE/CONDITIONS/SITUATIONS TO GOD

As we have proceeded through this workbook and Florence's book we've learned of the power of releasing people/conditions/situations to God – the power of forgiveness and the power of non-resistance.

We are each a spiritual being, but we are also human. The human side of us does not want to let go or to release our control of people, conditions or situations to anybody – especially not to someone we cannot see. How can we trust God to take care of anything?

God created the universe, flowers, water, air, animals and us. He developed the complicated envelope we call our bodies. He can handle whatever it is we have going on in our lives.

Most of the time, resolving an issue comes down to the fact that we have nothing to lose by truly releasing all to God. It is then, in that moment of release that the universe goes into full swing and is able to match to us what we truly desire.

WORKBOOK ITEM THREE

This exercise is designed to help you release any lingering fears as well as fears that have just been revealed to you. Sit quietly and look within. Look within honestly. Are you holding on to unforgiveness with someone? With yourself? Are there lingering doubts as to your limitlessness? Is there an area with fear that has just been revealed? If so, identify the fear and use The Sedona Method® of Release or the Healing Circle of Love to transmute the fear source to love.

Use the Journal Page to write about your experience – make note as to where your weaknesses are, if you have any, such as finances or relationships. Now you not only have the tools to recognize where and what the weaknesses are, but you have the tools to heal them.

JOURNAL PAGE:

VISUALIZING AND VISIONING

Florence explains visualizing and visioning in the following manner:

Visualizing is a mental process governed by the reasoning or conscious mind.

Visioning is a spiritual process, governed by intuition, or the superconscious mind.

As we progress in our bonding connection with our God Part within through meditation and quiet conversations, we will become privy to visions of our gifts and/or our mission. We will be guided to steps to take to bring the visions into our reality.

Visualizing is a powerful tool to manifest our desires. Visualizing what we truly desire in our lives will anchor it in the universe, giving the universe a clear understanding of the vibrational frequency that it must match.

WORKBOOK ITEM FOUR

This exercise is designed to help you expand your feelings of limitlessness and experience in your mind the desires of your heart.

Visualization Form

1. Discern what you truly want. Write here what it is.
2. Visualize experiencing what it is that you want. Apply the statements that are appropriate to your desire. Visualize how it feels, how it looks, what it tastes like, what you look like wearing it, how it smells, is it cold? is it hot? Visualize experiencing your desire with all your senses. Write about what you desire here – be specific in detail.

3. On a scale of one to ten, where did your experience of receiving your desire fall? If it is less than 10, repeat number 2 till it is a 10. Experience the gratitude of the visualization. Place it in your archive of Gratitude Attraction Magnets – as if you have already received.

4. Spend a few minutes each day visualizing the joy and gratitude of experiencing receipt of your desire or something better. Experience the gratitude of having received under grace in a perfect way. Where do you feel the receipt of your visualization?

Use the Journal Page to write of this experience. Write about the outcome. Did you bring to fruition your desire? Or did you negate it with doubt and worry? Write about what you learned.

JOURNAL PAGE:

RULES: FEARLESS FAITH, NON-RESISTANCE AND LOVE!

Florence's goal in *The Game of Life* is to help man free himself of physical world conditioning and beliefs. She set forth guidelines, examples and now through this workbook, tools of experiential exercises to realign man's thinking with that of God in the Fourth Dimensional Realm.

The tools are here to *"bring into manifestation the 'Divine Design of his life, Health, Wealth, Love and Perfect Self-Expression.' 'Be ye transformed by the renewing of your mind."*

WORKBOOK ITEM FIVE

This is the final exercise of the Square of Life Today Form. You have experienced profound spiritual growth. Look at your square of life honestly. What does it reveal today? Read each section and write in the status of each.

My Square of Life Today Form

Health – A healthy physical body that houses our spirit
Love - Relationships that are fulfilling and love based
Perfect Self-Expression – Work that fulfills our passion that we love
Wealth – Cash flow that fulfills our needs and desires

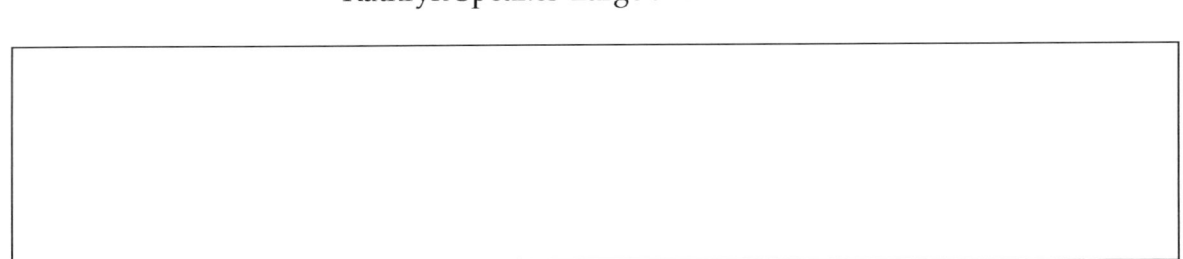

Compare this form to the one in Chapter One. Is your life the same? Have you grown tremendously? Are your desires coming to fruition? Do you have more love, more peace and more contentment in your life? Are you freer? Use the Journal Page to write about your discoveries.

Remember, good things in your life are ***not rewards for good behavior*** – each one of us is a profoundly loved child of God. It is our birthright to receive good things – Prosperous Abundance in the Square of Life. God, Infinite Spirit, The Creator, Our Heavenly Father, is a loving God who has great abundance for each one of us, it is up to us to use our free will wisely and allow ourselves to receive that abundance.

JOURNAL PAGE:

RECAP

Before reading Florence Scovel Shinn, many of us were struggling and living our lives from a totally unconscious level. We were simply surviving from day to day, from pay check to pay check. In reality, we were choosing to make our lives a struggle.

Now we have learned how truly powerful and limitless we are.

We now have tools to help us discern our mission of service to the world and to God. We have gained an inner knowing of ourselves that had eluded us before.

We've connected with the God Part within and learned to work in harmony with our conscious, subconscious and our superconscious on an amazing level to bring to fruition the life we truly desire to live. We've learned how to purge from our lives the conditioning of the physical world and are now remembering *who we are!*

The door is open to live the life truly desired as One with God.

The Game of Life and How to Play it is filled with a tremendous amount of information. This workbook provides tools to understand more fully what Florence wrote about in 1926. Each time we read the book, we are elevated to a higher level of understanding, and we achieve a better grasp on the concepts within. Give yourself some time for all the information of the workbook to sink in, and then go through it again. You will find yourself at a higher level of understanding and will achieve an even better grasp on the concepts and tools.

Be sure to thank your guides, teachers and angels for being in attendance and helping you to clearly understand God's work.

May you be profoundly blessed in this moment and in every moment after...

JOURNAL PAGES:

JOURNAL PAGES continued:

Your Life has been Changed Forever - 2010, 2011 and 2012

Your life has changed forever. You'll never be able to go back to being the "follow the leader" person who floats around on the sea of life with no direction. Now you have tools to claim your power and create the life you truly desire to live.

Others will want to know what you've done. Share with them! Perhaps you'll be inspired to use this workbook to begin your own classes to help others create the life they truly desire!

What you will find with this book is that every time you pick it up you will learn more, for you will be at a higher level of evolvement and will understand yet more of the true essence of the work. Personally I've picked up The Game of Life hundreds of times and each time I learn more and "get" what Florence is teaching at a greater depth. The experience is always nothing short of miraculous.

This workbook holds tools of tremendous power – use them!

You are a magnificent, limitless, profoundly loved spiritual being with a Field of Potentiality and Possibilities that will leave you in awe when you open the way to tap into it. Nothing is too big or too good for you – remember this!

There will be follow-up editions of this workbook for 2011 and 2012. Each one will be more highly evolved with more insights and tools.

Go forth and be the spiritual being Mother Earth desires living prosperously from a source of love…

May you be profoundly blessed in this moment and in every moment after…

In love and light,

Kate

The Sedona Method® of Release

This procedure is shockingly simple and extremely powerful! It is based upon The Sedona Method® releasing technique, a simple way to let go of any negative thoughts, feelings or emotions that may arise and is printed with permission of Sedona Training Associates, Sedona.com. The purpose of the following procedure is to release completely negative beliefs and/or thought patterns that are blocking your receipt of abundance from God.

Make yourself comfortable; ask your guides and angels to surround you with God's Divine White Light. Breathe slowly and deeply to help you focus within.

The following exercise is based upon The Sedona Method® and
is printed with permission of Sedona Training Associates. Sedona.com

Step 1: Focus on one of the negative beliefs or thought patterns you have about yourself that you discovered in the previous exercise. Allow yourself to experience and feel FULLY the negative-ness of the belief or thought pattern. Embrace the negative feelings of the belief or thought pattern. Welcome the negativity into your body freely and completely.

It sounds counter productive to "embrace" something that you are trying to "release," but it isn't. By fearlessly embracing the negative beliefs and thought patterns you show active faith of your safety within God – you are facing your fears. You are actually releasing the negativity by embracing it into the God Part within you!

Step 2: Ask yourself: Could I let this feeling go? Answer the question honestly with the first answer that comes to you – "yes" or "no." No matter what the answer, try again to embrace the feeling to you – can you find the feeling? Embrace it to you. Go on to Step 3 no matter how you answered the question.

Step 3: Ask yourself: Would I let this feeling go? Answer the question honestly with the first answer that comes to you – "yes" or "no." No matter what the answer, try again to embrace the feeling to you – can you still find the feeling within you? If so, embrace it to you. Go on to Step 4 no matter how you answered the question.

Step 4: Ask yourself: When will I let this feeling go? Answer the question honestly. This question gives you the opportunity to completely dissipate the feeling NOW.

Step 5: Repeat this procedure as often as necessary to be completely free of the negative-ness.

It stands to reason that when your goal is to release the negative feeling, you would try to release it, not embrace it. However, in executing the act of "embracing" the feeling, you are in reality releasing it through the God Part within us. Through this God Part the negativity dissipates in Love.

Move through each section of the square of life releasing negative feelings with The Sedona Method® of release. Write in your journal the negative belief or thought pattern and your experience in releasing it.

After you have experienced this exercise you will understand how amazingly powerful the procedure is.

The Healing Circle of Love
as Given by Princess Diana and Mother Teresa

The following is a powerful guided meditation to aid you in shifting from a source of fear to a source of love to heal inharmony within you.

Healing Circle of Love as given by Princess Diana and Mother Teresa

Blessings to you and welcome to a Healing Circle of Love.

Together we set the intention to connect with the angelic realm of love.

In order to open the channels of communication to the highest level, breathe deeply, fully and completely, filling the entire body with oxygen, not just the lungs.

And so we begin… With the highest of intentions we pray…

Father, Mother God, Creator of All That Is…

Surround us with your divine white light of healing love and allow only those spirits of God to connect with us. We ask for your presence to help us pull from within the divine love of you, our creator. May this love dissipate our fear and shift us to the glorious state of love. May this love permeate our being with peace and gratitude. Bless this divine intention to connect with the source of love.

In deepest gratitude,

AMEN.

Throughout this journey continue to breathe deeply. Focus on the experience of the breath as it enters the body – Take a slow deep breath in… slowly exhale. Breathe deeply and hold for a count of three, then slowly exhale.

Breathe in deeply, hold for a count of three, then slowly exhale.

See your self surrounded with God's white light. Breathe in the love of the Divine light. As you breathe deeply you experience a slight swirling mist in the light. You feel it gently touch your face, soft and fluid as the gentle embrace of angel wings.

Exhale the challenges and hiccups of the physical world. Focus fully on the breath as it enters the body expanding the lungs fully and completely.

As you breathe in deeply of the gentle swirling mist of light, you begin to feel the love...

As you are focusing on your breath, notice there are roots beginning to extend from your feet out across Mother Earth. These roots burrow into the soil of mother earth deeper and deeper, down through the rocks, the water, the clay, down deep into Mother Earth. Upon reaching the center of Mother Earth you see a brilliant glowing ball of light. The roots from your feet infuse into this ball of light energy.

As you breathe deeply, pull this vibrant energetic light back up through the roots – through the clay, the water, the rocks and the soil; back up into your feet. The energy travels up through your feet, up through your legs, up through your chakras.

As it travels up through your body, feel the tingle of recognition and excitement at the familiar properties of the energy. You are One with Mother Earth – One with The Creator of All That is...

As the energy reaches the top of your head, with your eyes still closed, gently allow your eyes to roll up as if to see this energy. You move with this energy out through the top of your head, out to blend with The Creator of All That Is.

Take a deep breath in... Before you is a pathway to a large beautifully carved door. You follow the pathway to the door. When you reach the door, you grasp the doorknob and turn it – the door opens easily. Go through the door and close it firmly behind you.

As you look around, you notice you are in a beautiful flower garden. This garden is filled with warm healing sunshine. All around you are brilliant, fragrant flowers with the most vibrant colors. In the center of the garden is a chair. Walk over to this chair and sit down.

When you are comfortable in the chair close your eyes and focus on the person or life situation you have chosen to heal with love during this journey.

While keeping this person or situation in mind, ask your angelic entourage to send to you angelic beings to help you.

Slowly open your eyes to see who has joined you. Is it someone you know? A deceased loved one, or an angel or ascended master? They are offering their hands to you. Rise and take their hands in yours. Together you form a circle with your loved one or life situation in the middle.

Pull forth from deep within you – love. Release feelings of worry, angst, fear and anger. Focus on the love. Allow this love to move through you and expand from you, moving to the loved one or life situation. Your angelic helpers are doing the same.

As you stand there holding hands with the angelic and holding the light of love together you become a glowing light – together. From above a ray of loving light gently flows into the center of your circle encompassing the person and/or life situation. Allow this love light to surround you and immerse you, permeating your being. Your angelic helpers do the same – you fuse together as one.

Allow the shift into love to be. The love bond is united and a calm peacefulness is yours. You feel the unforgiveness dissipate within you – allow the love to take its place. You forgive yourself. Harsh feelings of anxiety and strife are dissipating – fear dissipates. All there is, is love – sweet, gentle love flowing throughout your body from head to toe.

Allow the love to fill you, breathe deeply of the loving light. Continue to breathe deeply and rejoice at the love. Allow yourself to see, feel and hear this angelic gift.

You are love…

You are one with God.

Peace is yours.

Take a few moments to to experience the gift of love…

Embrace the love of this experience. You have discovered the sense of peace within you. The angst of worry, stress and fear will have dissipated. If you find remnants of it still lurking within, ask your angelic helpers to help you continue to dissolve it. They will increase the flow of love and light.

As you release each other's hands, notice the love stays with you – each of you continue to glow softly of love. Thank your angelic assistants for helping you to shift from fear to love. Allow the peace of this love to be yours. Embrace it.

Now you must return to the physical world. Say goodbye to your angelic assistants and retrace your steps back to the door of the garden. Go through the door - closing it firmly behind you and follow the pathway back to your physical world space.

Notice the roots at your feet once again extend out into the soils of Mother Earth, down through the rocks, the water, the clay to the brilliant glowing light at the center of Mother Earth. The roots infuse with the light and pull it back up through the clay, through the water, through the rocks, through the soils of Mother Earth back to the bottom of your feet. The healing energy moves up through your legs to your heart chakra and stops. You are grounded and fully returned to the physical world.

Breathe deeply and completely. Allow yourself to bask in the glow of this blessed journey. Embrace fully the shift to love.

Sacred Space ~ Build it and They Will Come

The following is a guided meditation to aid you in connecting with your angelic entourage of angels, guides, teachers and deceased loved ones.

Sacred Space ~ Build It and They Will Come

Blessings to you and welcome to Sacred Space ~ Build it and They Will Come

Together we set the intention to connect with the spiritual being of your choice. We are seeking wisdom, guidance and above all to meld our souls with God, thereby rejuvenating and replenishing our essence with the love of His holy presence.

Breathing is the acknowledgement that we are still willing to live in the physical world. In so doing, we connect with God and the angels without thinking about it. In order to open the channels of communication to the highest level, breathe deeply and completely, filling the entire body with oxygen, not just the lungs.

And so we begin… With the highest of intentions we begin with a prayer…

Father, Mother God, Creator of All That Is…

Surround us with your divine white light of healing love and allow only those spirits of God to connect with us. We ask for your presence to enlighten us, to share your wisdom and guidance, to rejuvenate and refresh our earthly bodies, to feel the peaceful joy of your love and to understand completely that we are your valuable children – one with God. Bless this divine intention to connect with the spirit realm.

In deepest gratitude,

AMEN.

Throughout this journey continue to breathe deeply. Focus on the experience of the breath as it enters the body – Take a slow deep breath in… slowly exhale. Breathe deeply and hold for a count of three, then slowly exhale.

Breathe in deeply, hold for a count of three, then slowly exhale.

See your self surrounded with God's white light. Breathe in the love of the Divine light.

Exhale the challenges and hiccups of the physical world. Focus fully on the breath as it enters the body expanding the lungs fully and completely.

As you are focusing on your breath, notice there are roots beginning to extend from your feet out across Mother Earth. These roots burrow into the soil of mother earth deeper and deeper, down through the rocks, the water, the clay, down deep into Mother Earth. Upon reaching the center of Mother Earth you see a brilliant blue ball of light. The roots from your feet infuse into this ball of light energy.

As you breathe deeply, pull this vibrant energetic light back up through the roots – through the clay, the water, the rocks and the soil; back up into your feet. The energy travels up through your feet, up through your legs, up through your chakras.

As it travels up through your body, feel the tingle of recognition and excitement at the familiar properties of the energy. You are One with Mother Earth – One with The Creator of All That is...

As the energy reaches the top of your head, your crown chakra, with your eyes still closed, gently allow your eyes to roll up as if to see this energy. Your consciousness moves out through you're the top of your head, out to meet with The Creator of All That Is.

Take a deep breath in... Before you is a pathway to a large beautifully carved door. You follow the pathway to the door. When you reach the door, you grasp the doorknob and turn it – the door opens easily. Go through the door and close it firmly behind you.

As you look around, you notice you are in a lush garden with massive trees surrounding it. This garden is filled with healing sunshine, pleasantly warming you while a gentle breeze tickles your skin. You see beautiful flowers with the most vibrant colors. Your favorite flowers and more. They all have a light gentle fragrance that teases your senses. As you move through the garden of blessings, you see sweet butterflies play in and around the flowers, creating a peaceful, serene, welcoming space – your Sacred Space.

You notice that the garden includes a grassy area where you may run and play, because pain and restrictions of earth, don't exist here. You are free. Free to do as you please. Free to run, to skip, and to jump. As you travel this beautiful place, you feel profoundly loved. You become lighter, freer, and happier than you have ever felt. You feel the love of God surging through your body and soul. You are breathing in pure joy and you feel it in every fiber of your being. You glow - the elation is all encompassing. You're smiling, laughing, and feeling deep within you the full vigor of God's love for you.

As you turn to your right you see a gentle meandering stream. On the bank of the stream is a welcoming park bench. Walk over to the bench and sit down. You are safe and you are not alone – your guest has arrived… You welcome them. Talk with them now – they've come to see you. Breathe deeply and visit…

Take the time you need to visit. When you are finished with your visit, graciously thank your visitor for meeting with you. You may schedule another meeting if you wish.

Now you must return to the physical world. Say goodbye to your visitor and follow the pathway back to the door of the garden. Go through the door - closing it firmly behind you and follow the pathway back to your physical world space.

Notice the roots at your feet once again extend out into the soils of Mother Earth, down through the rocks, the water, the clay to the brilliant blue light at the center of Mother Earth. The roots infuse with the light and pull it back up through the clay, through the water, through the rocks, through the soils of Mother Earth back to the bottom of your feet. The healing energy moves up through your legs to your heart chakra and stops. You are grounded and fully returned to the physical world.

Breathe deeply and completely. Notice you feel refreshed and rejuvenated. In this moment, you are complete love and you feel it throughout your body.

Claim Your Power

The following is a guided meditation to aid you in claiming your personal power.

Claim Your Power ~ Create the Life of Your Dreams!

Blessings to you and welcome to the Claim Your Power and create the life of your dreams meditation!

Together we set the intention to embrace your Power and stimulate your energy! We will claim and embrace the exuberant joy of stepping fully into your power and raise your vibrational frequency to that of the angelic realm of love.

In order to open the channels of communication to the highest level, breathe deeply, fully and completely, filling the entire body with oxygen.

And so we begin… With the highest of intentions we begin with a prayer…

Father, Mother God, Creator of All That Is…

Surround us with your divine white light of healing love and allow only those spirits of God to connect with us. We ask for your presence to help us pull from within the divine love of you, our creator. May this love dissipate our fear and shift to a state of joy as we claim and embrace our personal power. Bless this divine intention to connect as One with you.

In deepest gratitude,

AMEN.

Throughout this journey continue to breathe deeply. Focus on the experience of the breath as it enters the body – Take a slow deep breath in… slowly exhale. Breathe deeply and hold for a count of three, then slowly exhale.

Breathe in deeply, hold for a count of three, then slowly exhale.

Breathe in deeply, fully and completely, then slowly exhale.

See your self surrounded with God's white light. Breathe in the love of the Divine light. As you breathe deeply you begin to see a swirl of golden light around you. This light gently explodes into golden mist. You feel it gently touch your face, soft and fluid as the gentle embrace of familiar love – the love of the angelic realm – of God.

Breathe in this loving gentle golden mist.

Breathe in deeply and exhale the challenges and hiccups of the physical world. Focus fully on the breath as it enters the body expanding the lungs fully and completely.

Breathe in deeply the gentle swirling mist of golden light. Relax into the light.

As you are focusing on your breath, notice there are roots beginning to extend from your feet out across Mother Earth. These roots burrow into the soil of mother earth deeper and deeper, down through the rocks, down through the water, down through the clay, down deep into Mother Earth. Upon reaching the center of Mother Earth you see a brilliant glowing ball of golden light. Breathe deeply, fully and completely as the roots from your feet infuse into this ball of golden light energy.

As you breathe deeply, pull this vibrant energetic golden light back up through the roots – through the clay, the water, the rocks and the soil; back up into your feet. The energy travels up through your feet, up through your legs, up through your body.

As it travels up through your body, feel a golden tingle of joy at reconnecting with the powerful essence of God - You are One with Mother Earth – One with The Creator of All That Is…

As the energy reaches the top of your head, with your eyes still closed, gently allow your eyes to roll up as if to see this energy. You move with this energy out through the top of your head, out to blend with The Creator once again fully One with God and All That Is.

Take a deep cleansing breath in… Before you is a pathway to a large beautiful golden door. You follow the pathway to the door. When you reach the door, you see there is a HUGE golden sun engraved on the door. The doorknob is a large diamond. You grasp the diamond doorknob and turn it – the door opens easily and warm sunshine spills through to gently embrace you. Go through the door and close it firmly behind you.

As you look around, you see you are in a lush, beautiful land. Before you is a golden pathway leading up a slight incline. The pathway is lined with beautiful, fragrant flowers of nature.

You feel welcome HERE!

Place one foot in front of the other and follow the golden path up the incline. Feel the excitement and joy at being here!

As you reach the top of the incline, the path levels off to an overlook of your limitless Field of Potentiality. Spread before you in a beautiful valley is everything you dream of. Yes……. If you can dream it, it is in your Field of Potential.

Breathe deeply – you are home! Gaze over the Field of Potentiality…. What do you see? Do you see good healthy? A new home? A new car? Do you see exciting work and career? Exciting vacations? Do you see loving relationships? Nothing is too big to dream – you see it all!

Breathe deeply and take a few moments to see and explore your dreams – your Field of Potentiality.

Breathe deeply and embrace the gratitude of the experience.

Now we are going to claim our personal power.

Breathe deeply and raise your arms up – stretching your hands out to the sky and shout,

"I embrace my Personal Power!"

It felt good, didn't it?

Now shout again, from deep within your being, *"I claim my Personal Power!"*

Embrace to you the exhilarating feeling of your power. Pull it into your heart. Feel the shift within you as you vibrate with the love of your power.

Breathe into it and shout one more time… *"I claim my Personal Power!"*

Now allow your eyes to sweep across your Field of Potentiality. Embrace to you the dreams that you see and claim them.

With your arms held high, command:

"I claim all that is mine by Divine Right to come to me NOW Under Grace in a Wonderful Way!"

Feel the empowerment – breathe deeply into it. Embrace the exhilaration and exuberance of this power!

Notice to your left and to your right you've been joined by your crowd of angels, guides and teachers. They are your angelic entourage and they are applauding – look at your support group!

Feel the Huge smile on your face. Throw your hands out even father and one more time repeat and command:

"I claim my personal Power – I claim all that is mine by Divine Right to come to me Now Under Grace and in Wonderful Ways! Thank you!"

Your angelic entourage applauds even louder!

As you now step back from the edge overlooking your Field of Potentiality, the angels surround you and congratulate you.

Breathe deeply embracing fully and completely your personal power – you are One with God – limitless and empowered.

As you breathe deeply your personal power integrates fully into your being. You have claimed your power to create the life you desire. You are a powerful, limitless spiritual being. Now you will go forth empowered to fulfill your dreams.

You turn to follow the golden pathway back to the door – it is EASY to fearlessly stroll along the pathway with your angelic entourage fully empowered.

As you reach the door, you thank your crowd of angels, guides and teachers for sharing this blessed experience with you. They excitedly assure you they are always with you and available to help you with anything and everything – all you need do is ask.

As you face the door, you notice this side of the door has a huge golden sun engraved on it too welcoming your empowered self back to the physical world.

Grasp the diamond doorknob and open the door – golden sunlight again spills through the door to embrace you and welcome you back to the physical world – for now you have fully claimed your personal power and are ready to create the life you truly desire.

Go through the door and firmly close it behind you.

Notice the roots at your feet once again extend out into the soils of Mother Earth, down through the rocks, the water, the clay to the brilliant glowing golden light at the center of Mother Earth. The roots infuse with the golden light and pull it back up through the clay, through the water, through the rocks, through the soils of Mother Earth back to the bottom of your feet. The healing energy moves up through your legs to your heart chakra and stops. You are grounded and fully returned to the physical world.

Breathe deeply and completely. Allow yourself to bask in the glow of this blessed journey. Embrace fully your personal power.

If you need an energy boost during the day, visualize standing at your Field of Potential and throw out your arms and claim your power.

Before you to go sleep, stretch your arms out wide, claim your power and say thank you, falling asleep in gratitude.

Upon waking, gratefully visualize stepping on to the plateau overlooking your Field of Potential – stretch out your arms, claim your power and say thank you.

Now go forth, fully empowered creating the life you truly desire.

Physical World Tool Recommendations

Books:

30 Days to EveryDay Miracles by Jennifer Hoffman

A Still, Small Voice by Echo Bodine

Angelspeake, How to Talk With Your Angels by Barbara Mark and Trudy Griswold

Conversations with God by Neale Donald Walsch

Real Prosperity Using the power of Intuition to Create Financial and Spiritual Abundance by Lynn A. Robinson

The Four Spiritual Laws of Prosperity by Edwene Gaines

The Seven Spiritual Laws of Success by Deepak Chopra

Waiting in the Other Room by Kathryn Speakes-Large

Meditation Tool:

Sacred Space ~ Build It and They Will Come Guided Meditation by Kathryn Speakes-Large Claim Your Power Guided Meditation by Kathryn Speakes-Large available

Release/Dissipate Fear Tool:

The Sedona Method® of Release: Sedona.com

The Healing Circle of Love as given by Princess Diana and Mother Teresa by Kathryn Speakes-Large

Daily Tools of Support:

Daily Spiritual Affirmation – a Soul Kiss Subscription SoulKisses.com

Guided meditations by Kathryn Speakes-Large are available: SoulKisses.com, CDBaby.com and FlorenceScovelShinnsGameOfLife.com

About the Author

Kathryn (Kate) Speakes-Large is an author, medium, teacher, photographer of orbs and a spiritual webmaster. She is a healer of the light with human words and a conduit for the comfort of God's healing love. She is certified and a master of several healing modalities that she uses to infuse love into all that she shares with others.

Kate works directly with her angelic entourage to bring tools, messages, comfort and love to the world through Soul Kisses Spiritual Whispers. She works closely with Jesus to share the Soul Kisses website as a healing tool to help others find the light within them as well as their truth, peace, comfort and love. It is a place for those who are searching for more to begin or continue their connection with their angels, guides - God. A place to discover, acknowledge and accept that we are never alone - we are indeed a crowd...

Kate's work is always changing, ascending and gifting her with enlightenment, peace and love. Jesus has shared with her that the website will provide light for the spiritual paths of multitudes. The ascension of the collective consciousness of the planet is shifting at great speed. The human spirits are recognizing there are messages within them they have forgotten - messages that must be pulled forth to remember and to experience the connection with The Creator. Kate's work with Jesus through the websites provides tools to aid the human spirits in this ascension.

Kate is also a spiritual webmaster. She has over 20 years of administrative and secretarial experience and has been designing websites since 1999. In 2001 she left the corporate world to work in her private office offering virtual assistance to clients throughout the US, Canada and China. Almost immediately the work took an unexpected, but exciting turn from virtual assistance to spiritual web design. To create the spiritually based websites she infuses the energy and essence of the client and their work into the site so the world clicking in will feel the quintessence of the work of the client. You may learn more about Kate's work by clicking into the SoulKisses.com, SpiritOrbPhotoOp.com, WebDesignsByKate.com, FlorenceScovelShinsGameOfLife.com and WaitingInTheOtherRoom.com websites.

Made in the USA
Charleston, SC
26 March 2010